God does work in history. He is the Lord
of history as He brings to pass each chapter
in His story of redemption. For centuries
before the birth of Jesus, God had been
preparing the world for that
great event. Without even knowing it, nations had
moved on and off the scene, fulfilling the
parts God planned. Then, "when the right
time finally came, God sent his own Son. . . .
so that we might become God's
sons" (Galatians 4:4,5).

MEN WHO KNEW CHRIST

By William Sanford LaSor

A Division of G/L Publications
Glendale, California, U.S.A.

Scripture quotations from the Revised Standard Version of
the Bible. Copyrighted 1946 and 1952, Division of Christian
Education, N.C.C.C., U.S.A. Used by permission.

The publishers do not necessarily endorse the entire contents of all publications referred to in this book.

Second Printing, 1971

Published by
Regal Books Division, G/L Publications
Glendale, California 91209, U.S.A.

Library of Congress Catalog Card No. 70-135026
ISBN 0-8307-0086-2

Contents

Preface

Names make news, we are told; and likewise, persons make history. We believe in a personal God who has dealt, even as He deals today, with persons.

In my first volume, *Men Who Knew God,* I attempted to tell the Old Testament story of God's redemptive activity through some of the significant personalities of Israel, His chosen people. Now in this account my aim is to tell the founding story of the Christian church by recounting the stories of some key New Testament personalities.

For centuries before the birth of Christ, God had been preparing the world for the advent of the Redeemer. Without being aware of it, nations moved on and off the scene, fulfilling the parts that were foreordained for them by God. All the nations were involved. The parts played in the divine plan by Egypt and

Assyria, Babylonia and Persia are familiar enough. But it is a gross mistake to assume that when the Old Testament story ends (in the fifth century B.C.), God's activity in history stopped and did not continue until the annunciation of the birth of Jesus.

Actually, some of the Lord's most important preparation of the world for Christ's coming was taking place in the centuries between the Old Testament and the New Testament. This book gives you a glimpse into those significant years, then moves on to see God working with men in New Testament times.

It is my sincere desire and prayer that this work will help you to know men who knew Christ—not just to know about them—and that as you come to know them as friends you will come to know better the God they served.

Prologue

PART I

The Fullness of Time

If you were going to launch a worldwide movement, when would you do it? You would probably wait until the political factors were just right. The ideal time would be when there was no war, and when communication was easy to all parts of the world. You would wait until the cultural factors were right. You would desire a minimum language barrier. You would look for ease in the spreading of ideas. And if the movement you were to launch happened to be a religious movement, you would feel that even the religious scene needed to be prepared.

In the letter to the Galatians, Paul says, "But when the time had fully come"—or as it is in the King James Version, "when the fullness of the time was come"— "God sent forth his Son, born of woman, born under the law, to redeem those who were under the law, so that we might receive adoption as sons" (Galatians

1

4:4f). In other words, Paul is saying that the advent of Jesus Christ occurred at that moment of history that could be described as "the fullness of time."[1] Jesus Himself suggested that the fullness of time had come when He began His public ministry with the words, "The time is fulfilled, and the kingdom of God is at hand" (Mark 1:15).

God works in history. God is the Lord of history. These sayings are so commonplace that they have become clichés. Yet in a very real sense these commonplace sayings are true. For centuries God had been preparing the world for the advent of the Redeemer. Without ever being aware of it, nations moved on and off the scene, fulfilling the parts that were determined for them: is this not what Paul was trying to tell the learned men of Athens (cf. Acts 17:24-26)? Only one nation in the world had an intimate acquaintance with God and knew something of His purposes: that was the nation Israel. But it is written very clearly in the pages of the Old Testament that Israel was not the only nation in which God was active or through which God was bringing to pass His purpose. Through His prophets He made it very clear, as indeed He had done in the first promise to Abraham, that all of the nations of the world were involved in His redemptive activity (cf. Genesis 12:3; Isaiah 60:1-3).

All the nations of the world were involved—how?[2] Students of the Bible are familiar enough with the Egyptians and the Assyrians, the Babylonians and the Persians, and the parts they played in the divine plan. But the story of the Old Testament ends approximately in the middle of the fifth century B.C. It is a gross mistake to suppose that God's activity ended at that

2

same time and did not begin again until the annunciations of the births of John the Baptist and Jesus of Nazareth. Some of the most important preparation of the world was taking place in the centuries between the Old Testament and the New Testament.

The political preparation.   Instead of thinking of the Biblical world as spreading over parts of three continents, think of it as a geographical and cultural entity bordering on the eastern half of the Mediterranean Sea. Because of the mountains that extend across the northern portion from the Alps to the Himalayas, and the desert that stretches across the southern portion, plus the desert and seas of the eastern portion, communication between those parts of Europe, Asia, and Africa that border on the Mediterranean was far less difficult than communication to the remaining parts of any of the continents. This single area is the Bible world. Yet, it is still true that there are three distinct parts of the Bible world. There were Asiatics, Europeans, and Egyptians (to the last of which should be added, of course, the Libyans, Ethiopians, and others). Although the Egyptians were of great importance in the earlier portion of Old Testament history, by the time of the last centuries before Christ, Egypt was no longer of primary importance. The struggle was between the Asiatics and the Europeans.

It is possible to trace a shift of power, first from the Semitic peoples in Asia to the non-Semitic, and specifically to the Indo-European peoples in Asia; then from the Asiatic Indo-Europeans to the European Greeks. The night Babylon fell before the forces of Cyrus the Great the domination of Semitic empires came to an end. When Darius the Third was conquered by Alexander the Great, the world-empires of the Asiatic peoples came to an end and the world-empires of the Europeans began. Since that time, only twice in history have Asiatics seriously threatened the supremacy of the European powers: first in the time of Mohammed, when the Islamic forces spread across northern Africa and into the Iberian Peninsula, only to be stopped by Charles Martel at Tours (A.D. 732); the second time when Genghis Khan[3] swept westward into Europe to the Dnieper River in the early thirteenth century A.D. Both of these attempts, it will be noted, are considerably later than the time of Christ, and both of them failed.[4]

The rise of world empires is undoubtedly part of the political preparation employed in the idea of the fullness of time. At the end of the third millenium B.C., Sargon of Akkad had ideas of world empire when he called himself, "king of the four quarters of the earth." But this amounted to little more than a self-conferred honorary degree. The idea, however, seems to have been present in the minds of rulers who succeeded him, and at last in the days of the second Assyrian Empire it began to take on reality. Tiglath-pileser I (c.1118-1078 B.C.) provided considerable stimulus for its development, but the carrying out belongs really to the dynasty of Tiglath-pileser III (c.745-727 B.C.), including Shalmaneser V (c.727-722 B.C.), Sargon II of Assyria (722-705 B.C.), and Sennacherib (705-681 B.C.).[5] The Assyrian empire was indescribably cruel, and maintained its grasp not so much by means of wise and efficient government as by sheer brute force. With the destruction of Nineveh in 612 B.C., it

4

was replaced by the Babylonian empire of Nebuchadnezzar; but this empire was doomed to fall even before it arose, for it had come into existence by a coalition of powers and was unable to maintain the loyalty of its allies.

The Medo-Persian empire came into being by the destruction of Babylon in 539 B.C., and proceeded to establish a system of government which should have furnished sufficient cohesion to hold together an empire stretching from the Aegean Sea to the Indus River and including Egypt. But the Medo-Persian empire probably overextended itself by attempting to subdue the Scythians along the Danube, and later by attempting to conquer Athens and other parts of Greece. At the same time, we must recognize the fact that another power had arisen that was able to conquer the Medo-Persian empire.

Alexander the Great of Macedon had come to the throne and succeeded in whipping together the peoples of Greece, who had hitherto shown no remarkable unity. Moreover, he had established an ideal which struck fire. Quickly he moved across the world of his day, conquering the Medo-Persian empire and attempting even to extend its boundaries. Alexander died young, before the empire was really unified, and he bequeathed his empire to his four generals who soon reduced it to four and then three parts. By the end of the fourth century B.C. it would seem that the idea of world empire had come to an end.

This, however, was not to be. A new power had arisen in the west which, after it had overcome its only western rival, Carthage, on the northern coast of Africa,[6] turned its attention to the east, and by 63

B.C., Rome had taken over the lands of the eastern Mediterranean. While it is true that the Roman empire did not reach its greatest extent until the rule of Trajan (A.D. 117), it is also true that Roman rule extended over enough of the world of Jesus' day that it could be called "the whole world" (Luke 2:1).

The Romans were able to give to the world that unity and strength of government which was necessary for peace and for the rapid spread of the gospel. *Pax Romana* (Roman peace) was not only an ideal; it was a fact. Perhaps for the only time in the history of the world there was an extended period of universal peace. If Jesus Christ had come into the world one hundred years either side of the actual time of His advent, the story, from the historian's point of view, would have been far different. Alongside *Pax Romana* was *Lex Romana* (Roman law). The Roman empire in some way had learned to balance local autonomy and central authority, the rights of individuals and the rights of the state. So well was Roman law developed that the legal systems of the Western world are largely drawn from it.

We would not suggest that there were no problems. In order to maintain peace, the Roman empire had a standing army of a quarter-million men. True, the citizen army maintained by conscription had been replaced by a professional army. But armed forces are expensive, and taxes were imposed in the forms of customs, excise, inheritance, and sales taxes, usually collected by men who bought the office as a concession and then charged what they could get. Once every fourteen years a census or poll-tax was levied. These things were sources of annoyance and an occasional riot. But all-in-all, it was a time of peace and prosperity.

The cultural preparation. The empires which had preceded that of Alexander the Great were dead. It would not be possible to speak of a continuing Babylonian or Persian ideal, or any other. But the ideal of Alexander the Great, with the establishment of the Roman empire, was far from dead. That ideal can be summarized in one word: Hellenism. While this term can be used, and has been used, to cover many things, it will help us to think of it as the desire to give to the world the best of Greek life and thought. Alexander wanted to establish all over his empire centers of Greek culture, libraries that would house Greek writings, theaters that would present Greek drama and music. Cities named "Alexandria" sprang up all over the empire, and anyone who travels in the Near East will be duly impressed by the magnificence and geographical extent of Greek ruins. The library in Alexandria, Egypt, possessed over 500,000 volumes, and this was not the only library in the empire, for when it caught fire, Antony gave to Cleopatra 200,000 volumes from the library at Pergamum as replacement. It was Alexander's ideal also that a common language should unit the empire, and, of course, that would be Greek. One of the most dramatic ways in which Alexander attempted to put into effect his ideal was a mass wedding ceremony, held at Susa (one of the capitals of the Medo-Persian empire), where Alexander and his generals, and ten thousand of his soldiers, attempted to symbolize the marriage of Europe and Asia by taking Persian wives.[7] In some ways Alexander's expedition could be looked upon as scientific, somewhat as was Napoleon's expedition to Egypt many centuries later. Alexander took with him scholars, historians, geographers, and botanists. He built a fleet of ships at the mouth of the Indus River which was to explore the coast of the Persian Gulf; and he had other ideas which were considerably in advance of his day.[8] And the most completely Hellenized part of the empire outside Greece itself was Syro-Palestine![9]

When the Roman empire achieved supremacy, it is fortunate, or we prefer to say, providential, that there was no spirit of pan-Romanism. No effort seems to have been made to overthrow the Hellenistic ideals, to replace the Greek language with the Latin, or to develop an indigenous Roman culture. To expect the world to adopt a second universal language so soon would be to expect the impossible. Greek continued to be the language of the empire for several centuries. Moreover, the Romans were imitators rather than originators. Their art is largely Greek art, and other elements of their culture owe much to the Greeks who preceded them. Rome made a different type of contribution to the culture of the world; perhaps we could say it was more practical. Hellenism was an ideal. *Pax Romana* and *Lex Romana* were not ideals, they were realities; and because they were realities, the Hellenistic ideal was able to take even firmer root than it had, and the unity of which Alexander dreamed was realized in the Roman empire. Roman roads tied the empire together; Roman ships plied the lanes of the Mediterranean; the Roman postal system made rapid communication possible; Roman citizenship not only protected the rights of individuals who were citizens, but made possible widespread travel. At the same time, the principle of colonial home rule added a sense of significance and individual value.

But a sense of human value can cause trouble! When a slave, or an ex-slave, suddenly realizes, "I, too, am a man," he can cause all sorts of difficulty for those who want to be masters. Slavery was a great problem in the Roman empire. It has been estimated that one-third to one-half of the entire population were slaves. Life was cheap. A master who was displeased with the way his slave served the table could throw him to the fish. A mistress could permanently disfigure her servant whom she caught brushing her hair. Emperors might send hundreds, even thousands, of slaves into the arena to engage in mass slaughter—just for enter-tainment! But others were thinking about these things. If human life has value, how can it be destroyed so easily? When life is cheap, immorality is rampant. In particular, immorality of a sexual nature is encouraged when human beings are insignificant. Roman writers have left us full, frank accounts of their day.[10] But Roman writers were also rebelling against such condi-tions. Cicero's orations against Catiline in 63 B.C., once known by every Latin student, are only one example.

There is a nobler side, even in fallen men, for which we ought to thank God. Men were grappling with serious matters. They did not always come up with the right answers, but they were making interesting suggestions. We still study their philosophies and find much of value in them. This is not the place to discuss them; I simply want to point out one fact: when God was ready to send His gospel into the world, there were men ready to give it serious consideration.

The religious preparation. The four and a half centuries between the close of the Old Testament and the advent of Jesus Christ were years of great experience for the Jewish people. At the beginning of the sixth century B.C., they had been carried from Judah to Babylon in captivity. In 538 B.C., Cyrus the Great had granted to them the opportunity of returning to their land. Not all Jews, however, returned; as a matter of fact, some estimates of the number of Jews who seized the opportunity are as low as ten per cent.[11] Those who remained in exile made a new home for themselves. That home was the world. Such Jews were the "Diaspora," or the Jews of the Dispersion.[12]

Several things happened to the Jewish people in the Dispersion. For one thing, they developed a world view. Too long had they associated their God merely with the land of Palestine. By the rivers of Babylon they had wept because they had thought they could not sing the Lord's song in a foreign land (see Psalm 137:1-4). But now they had come to realize that the world was the Lord's. They not only could sing the Lord's song in foreign lands—they could even translate the song into foreign languages! In Babylon and the Mesopotamian region, as well as in the land of Egypt to which Jews had migrated in the time of Jeremiah and possibly earlier, Aramaic became the language of the Jewish people. Jews gradually spread to other parts of the world, and began to speak the Greek language. As their knowledge of the original Hebrew language decreased, it became increasingly necessary to have an explanation of the meaning of the Scriptures. Interpretations in Aramaic were at first preserved in oral form only, known as Targums, but later these were

standardized in written form. Likewise Greek translations of the Old Testament Scriptures were made,
which were far more significant for the New Testament
period than were the Aramaic Targums.

The Greek translations were important because the
Jewish people were undergoing, consciously or uncon-
sciously, a process of Hellenization. If they were not
all participating in the games in the stadium—some
indeed going so far as to have the visible signs of
circumcision removed by an operation—at least their
vocabulary was being expanded with Greek ideas.
When the Hebrew Old Testament was translated into
Greek, Hebrew words that had narrow meanings were
often translated by Greek words that had broader
meanings. Key theological terms had to be translated
by words that had various nuances and connotations
not present in the original. It could not possibly be
otherwise. Our words are integrally part of our culture.
When two cultures merge, the language has to become
richer.[13] And the Jews had entered the Hellenistic
stream of culture. The old wineskins were already being
stretched; the new wine would require new wineskins.
It is highly doubtful that Paul could have preached
his gospel in the Gentile world if he had been limited
to the concepts of the Hebrew Old Testament, and
certainly impossible if he had been limited to the
Hebrew language.

Another feature of the Dispersion was the development of the synagogue to serve as a partial substitute
for, and later to take the place of, the temple at
Jerusalem. While Jews lived in the land of Palestine,
it was possible to fulfill literally the law requiring
attendance at the annual feasts. When, because of

11

distance, this could no longer be fulfilled, the synagogue provided a means of religious expression. It also provided a means of community, so that the Jews of the Dispersion continued to use the Scriptures of the Old Testament, and to a lesser and modified extent they preserved the elements of worship. It does not need to be argued that the preachers of the gospel found their first steppingstones into the Gentile world in the synagogues scattered throughout that world.

An entire study could be devoted to the development of the Messianic expectation among the Jews, but here it is enough to point out that the hope that the day of deliverance was at hand was burning brightly. A whole literature was being produced centering largely about this theme.[14] False messiahs had arisen and would continue to arise for another century.

Nor was this sense of expectation limited to the Jews. There was in the Gentile world a sense of dissatisfaction with existing religions, and alongside this an expectation of something better. The Greeks had climbed Mount Olympus and found no gods there. The Latin writers Tacitus and Suetonius record the expectation of a powerful king.[15] All over the Gentile world many were becoming proselytes to Judaism, and it seems reasonable to suppose that it was the Messianic hope rather than the Mosaic law that was appealing to them.

This, then, is the fullness of time. God had prepared His world. Politically it was at peace under a stable government. Culturally it was united in the Greek language and the Hellenistic ideal. And the Jews, the people of God, scattered throughout the world, had at last come to the threshold and were ready to enter in to fulfill the promise made to Abraham, that they not only should be blessed, but that they should also be a blessing to the nations of the world.

Notes

1. For a stimulating discussion of "the fullness of time," see Otto Piper, *God in History* (New York: The Macmillan Company, 1939), pp. 1-40.

2. I have tried to show something of the historical activity of God in my previous volume, *Men Who Knew God*, William S. LaSor, Regal Book, G/L Publications, 1970.

3. Pronounced Jĕng′ gis kän′—it is a common mistake to pronounce the first g hard.

4. This is of course not to imply the superiority of the European over the Asiatic, nor for that matter over the African. The historian knows that there is no assurance that the Western powers will continue to maintain a relative supremacy in the world; in fact, the decline of the West was apparent to some historians years ago.

5. It is debatable whether this succession of kings should be called a dynasty. According to most scholars, Sargon was a usurper of the throne; on the other hand, van der Meer lists him as a brother of Shalmaneser V (cf. P. van der Meer, *The Chronology of Ancient Western Asia and Egypt* [2d ed.; Leiden: E. J. Brill, 1955], p. 76). Unfortunately, van der Meer does not document this, and I have been unable to find the record in which the relationship is expressed.

6. In the three Punic Wars, 264-241, 218-201, and 149-146 B.C.

7. Arrian, *Anabasis of Alexander*, 7.4.4-8; Plutarch, *Life of Alexander*, 70.2. It is true that Alexander's soldiers conducted a burning and looting expedition, and some scholars have little sympathy with Alexander's pan-Hellenic ideal; cf. A. T. E. Olmstead, *History of the Persian Empire* (Chicago: University of Chicago Press, 1948), pp. 519-523. The attitude of Ghirshman, reminding us of Voltaire's words ("Alexander had built more towns than other conquerors had destroyed"), is a moderating viewpoint; cf. R. Ghirshman, *Iran* (Pelican Book A239; Harmondsworth, Middlesex: Penguin Books, 1954), pp. 212-219.

8. S. Vernon McCasland has pointed out that this expansion of Greek influence had been under way for a long time and that Alexander's conquests only gave an impetus to it; cf. "The Greco-Roman World," in *The Interpreter's Bible* (New York: Abingdon-Cokesbury Press, 1951), vol. 7, p. 75. It is nevertheless true that the impetus was needed, and Alexander provided it.

9. Cf. John Pentland Mahaffy, *The Progress of Hellenism in Alexander's Empire* (Chicago: University of Chicago Press, 1905), p. 97.

10. For a graphic resumé, amply documented, see David R. Breed, *A History of the Preparation of the World for Christ* (New York: Fleming H. Revell Company, 1893), pp. 403-430. More restrained is McCasland's treatment, *art. cit.*, in *The Interpreter's Bible*, vol. 7, pp. 80-84. Paul refers to this condition in Romans 1:18-32.

11. See *Men Who Knew God*, pp. 182, 183.

12. Cf. F. J. Foakes Jackson and Kirsopp Lake, *The Beginnings of Christianity* (London: Macmillan and Co., 1922), vol. 1, pp. 137-168; and Robert H. Pfeiffer, *History of New Testament Times* (New York: Harper & Brothers, 1949), pp. 166-196. The latter has an excellent bibliography.

13. One very familiar illustration is our own English language, which after the Norman conquest absorbed many French words to take care of new cultural elements.

14. Cf. Charles F. Pfeiffer, *Between the Testaments* (Grand Rapids: Baker Book House, 1959), pp. 121-124; the entire book will provide an introduction to the intertestamental period. For a more detailed study, cf. Robert H. Pfeiffer, *op. cit.*, 561 pp.

15. Tacitus, *History*, 5.13; Suetonius, *Vespasian*, 4.

Prologue

PART II

Jesus the Son of Man

The birth of Jesus occurred in an unusual way. According to independent testimony, both Joseph and Mary were disturbed by the annunciations of the birth, for, as both records state clearly, there had been no union between them (Matthew 1:18 and Luke 1:34). By the Holy Spirit, Jesus was conceived in the womb of an intact virgin, hence we say He was "born of the virgin Mary." This is the historic faith of the Church.[1]

But when we have said that, let us remember that Jesus was born just as any other child. Once He was conceived in Mary's womb, the processes were the normal life processes. Mary carried the child as all mothers do. When the time came, she gave birth to the child as all mothers do.

Jesus was born in Bethlehem,[2] due to a census or poll tax that required Joseph to appear in his ancestral town. We do not know the year, and we do not know the day.[3] Yet the event was of sufficient importance that a star appeared, leading wise men from the East to worship the child-King (Matthew 2:1,2), and a king became so agitated that he caused the massacre of baby boys in Bethlehem (Matthew 2:16). The event one day changed the calendars of the world to read "Before Christ" and "In the Year of Our Lord."

Jesus grew up in Nazareth in Galilee. There were other children in the home. Four brothers are named: James, Joseph, Simon, and Judas; and there were also sisters (at least two; some think "all" means at least three—cf. Matthew 13:55,56). He lived a normal childhood; there is no place for the fantastic accounts we find in the apocryphal gospels. There we read that the boy Jesus made clay birds, then caused them to fly away; He stretched boards to the right length for Joseph; He carried water from the well in His cloak when He broke a pitcher; He made a salted fish come back to life. Even worse, we read that He cursed one teacher, ridiculed another, and struck dead a boy who accidentally bumped Him, until the parents of the city begged Joseph, "Take away that Jesus of yours from this place." Such stories are fantastic! The Church, Protestant and Catholic alike, has repudiated them.[4] There is no place for them historically or psychologically. When the time came for Jesus to take up His ministry, there is not the slightest indication that His fellow townspeople were either offended by His prior life or prepared for His miracles. They were simply amazed. "Where did this man get this wisdom and these mighty works? Is not this the carpenter's son?" (Matthew 13:54,55).

It was a poor home. Sometimes it seems that incidental details in Jesus' teaching came from watching His mother. "Why don't you sew a new patch on that?" "Why don't you put the new wine in those old wineskins?" "Why are you sweeping the corners of the room so carefully?" "Why do you use only such a little bit of leaven?"

There would come a time when He would learn to read. Perhaps He was sent to the synagogue school.[5] He doubtless learned Aramaic, the common tongue, and Hebrew, the holy tongue; and, living in Galilee of the Gentiles, He probably learned some common expressions in Greek.

He loved the world of nature. He observed the birds, the flowers, the sower and his seed, the fisherman and his net, the clouds and storms, the stifling, blasting wind from the desert.

There was a saying, "Who does not teach his son a trade teaches him to steal." Joseph taught Jesus the carpenter's trade. He learned to work with His hands and arms until, I am sure, His hands were calloused and His arms were muscular. These paintings hanging in the museums of the world that make Jesus look like an emaciated weakling do not give the true picture! He could tramp the hills of Palestine with rugged men and keep up with the best of them.

He knew the Scriptures. He knew how to pray. He took part in the religious festivals, and it was His custom to attend synagogue on the Sabbath. When He visited Jerusalem in His twelfth year, perhaps for the *bar mitzvah* ceremony when He would take His

17

place as a man in Israel, He amazed the doctors of the Law with His understanding and His answers. And He did not get those answers by being the Son of God! He got them by studying, just as you and I have to study. Then He went back to Nazareth with His parents "and he was obedient to them."

We know little of the eighteen years that follow, the "hidden years." We know that Jesus worked in the carpenter shop. It is quite probable that Joseph died, and that Jesus became the breadwinner of the family. We can be certain that He lived a perfectly normal life, from the reaction of the people; we can also be certain that He lived a perfectly pure life, from the reaction of God who said, "This is my beloved Son, with whom I am well pleased" (Matthew 3:17).

The beginnings of Jesus' ministry. One day, when John the Baptist had been baptizing for possibly six months, and the people were stirred to excitement by him, Jesus went from Galilee to the Jordan to be baptized by John. When John saw Jesus, he protested, "I need to be baptized by you, and do you come to me?" (Matthew 3:14). Did John know Jesus? John says, "I myself did not know him" (John 1:31). What was it then that made John protest? Perhaps it was the clean appearance of One who had never sinned. At any rate, Jesus said, "Let it be so now; for thus it is fitting for us to fulfil all righteousness" (Matthew 3:15). Certainly Jesus was not baptized in repentance for His own sins for He had none; He was baptized because He wanted to take His place with you and me. There was to be nothing to separate Him from the people He came to save.[6]

Following the baptism, John testified that he saw a dove descending upon Jesus, the sign that this was indeed the One for whom John was to prepare the way (cf. John 1:32-34).

Immediately, Jesus was driven into the wilderness to be tempted by the devil (cf. Luke 4:1-13). He was tempted as man; He faced both the subtle and the bold attacks of the tempter in exactly the same way that you and I must face them. We get our ideas of sin hopelessly confused at times. We stress the fact that it is inherited, and we forget the fact that the greatest sin comes from our own hearts, our own wills. The great battleground of sin is in the human will. It is not the *temptation* that is sin, but what we will to do under temptation. It is not even the *deed*, but what we *will* to do. We may for one reason or another restrain the action; but the very fact that *we would like to do it* is sin. (Read carefully Matthew 5:21-30.) When Jesus met the tempter, He met him in the same freedom of will that you and I have as human beings. Moreover, Jesus faced the temptations under the worst possible conditions: in the wilderness, and alone.

There is no evidence that Jesus' temptations ended at that time. Rather, it seems that He constantly faced temptation, for He "in every respect has been tempted as we are, yet without sinning" (Hebrews 4:15). On the last night of His earthly life, in the garden of Gethsemane, when He knew that He must drain the cup of death to its bitter dregs, He prayed in great agony, "My Father, if it be possible, let this cup pass from me" (Matthew 26:39). Not once, but three times He prayed this prayer. And every time He countered it with the prayer, "Nevertheless, not as I will, but as thou wilt." This was the greatest temptation He ever faced: the temptation to save Himself. But He knew that if He saved Himself, He could never save others.

Jesus and His disciples. There is a saying, that if you would know a man, eat with him and sleep with him. Jesus ate and slept with His disciples. There are many teachers who get up in the morning, wash and put on their better clothes, go into the classroom or lecture hall and deliver their carefully prepared lecture, and then go back home. Their students may never know how they live.

But Jesus did not teach that way. He did not get His disciples together for an hour or two a day in a lecture hall. He lived with them. They saw Him under all conditions: when He was hungry, passing through a field of grain; when He was tired, stretched out in the boat. They saw Him when religious officialdom prodded Him with sticky questions; they saw Him when a sinful woman washed His feet with tears of devotion because her sins had been forgiven. They saw Him bless little children; they saw Him drive money changers out of the Temple. They saw Him under every possible condition that could occur for about a year or more. Then one day Jesus said to them, "Who do you say that I am?" Peter spoke up, "You are the Christ, the Son of the living God" (Matthew 16:15,16).

Jesus taught His disciples. Wonderful teachings! He used simple language, and drew upon familiar things for illustrations, and yet His teachings are so inexhaustible that men are still writing books about them, trying to get at the root of what Jesus taught. The subjects are of primary importance. Jesus is talking about God, about man, about sin and salvation, about righteousness and justice, about love and forgiveness. He is talking about the great central truths of life, the foundational matters on which all human relationships are built.[7] Little wonder that, when they listened to Him, they were astonished, "for he taught them as one who had authority, and not as their scribes!" (Matthew 7:29). Little wonder that they said, "No man ever spoke like this man!" (John 7:46).

Jesus and His Father.　　Have you ever thought about Jesus and His Father? You probably have discussed the relationship between the First and Second Persons of the Trinity, but have you ever thought about the relationship between Jesus as a human being and His heavenly Father? In Philippians, Paul presents a subject that has evoked much discussion: theologians call it "kenosis." Speaking of Christ Paul says: "who, though he was in the form of God, did not count equality with God a thing to be grasped, but emptied himself, taking the form of a servant, being born in the likeness of men. And being found in human form he humbled himself and became obedient unto death, even death on a cross" (Philippians 2:6-8). This "emptying" is the kenosis. I do not pretend to know all that it means, but I am sure that it means at least this: while Jesus was in human form He had the same relationship with God that you and I have as human beings.[8]

How did Jesus get along with God on this basis? It stands out clearly in the Scripture record: He pleased God. At the time of the baptism, that is, after about thirty years of life, He heard God say, "Thou art my

21

beloved Son; with thee I am well pleased" (Mark 1:11). On the Mount of Transfiguration, when the public ministry of Jesus was all but over and He was about to set His face to go to Jerusalem, God declared again, "This is my beloved Son, with whom I am well pleased" (Matthew 17:5). Jesus could look His fellow men in the eyes and say, "which of you convicts me of sin?" (John 8:46), and He could stand before God and say unashamed and unafraid, "I always do what is pleasing to him" (John 8:29). He could pray, "Thy will be done," knowing that He would be happy with that will. When some of us pray "Thy will be done," I think we keep our fingers crossed!

On the last night of His earthly life, knowing that the next few hours would bring His death, He could say to God, "I glorified thee on earth, having accomplished the work which thou gavest me to do. . . . I have manifested thy name to the men whom thou gavest me. . . . I kept them in thy name. . . . I have given them thy word" (John 17:4, 6, 12, 14). He could look into His Father's face as He hung on the cross and say, "It is finished. . . . into thy hands I commit my spirit" (John 19:30; Luke 23:46).

This is how Jesus got along with God His Father. Do you want proof? Here it is: God raised Him from the dead. God has not raised anyone else from the dead.[9] But God, by the resurrection of Jesus Christ from the dead, said in effect, "This One does not deserve to die!" Therefore, Paul says, Jesus was "designated Son of God in power"—or it might be translated, "marked out as" or "declared to be the Son of God in power"—"by his resurrection from the dead" (Romans 1:4).[10]

There is another nature about which we have said practically nothing: the divine nature of Jesus. Yet that was also manifest during His earthly life and ministry. We have not mentioned His knowledge of the inner-most thoughts of men, nor His power to work miracles. These things were not used by Jesus to call attention to Himself, but only in the service of His fellow men. We have said far too little about His redemptive work, His substitutionary death, His resurrection and ascension, and His sending of the Holy Spirit. We have not mentioned the great purifying hope of the Church, the return of Jesus Christ. But these cardinal truths are so woven into the lives of the men yet to be considered, that we shall not ignore them.

We have confined our study to Jesus the man. He is the perfect man, the Adam who did not fall. He is the living proof that God's will is not impossible. If, in the judgment, Adam wants to stand up and say to his Creator, "You gave me something that could not possibly be done!" God can point to His Son who emptied Himself of His glory and took upon Himself Adam's likeness, who was tempted in all points as Adam was, without sinning, and God can say with finality, "He did it!"

But someone says, "I am not Adam; I inherited from Adam a fallen nature. I can't please God." Are you going to hide behind that excuse? God sent Jesus Christ into the world in order that we might hide behind Him and not behind Adam. In Christ that old man is crucified; you are a new man in Christ. No longer is Adam your example; now your example is Christ, that you should walk as He walked.[11]

But He is not a heartless and cold example, ready

to destroy us if we fall. He is our help and encouragement. "Because he himself has suffered and been tempted, he is able to help those who are tempted" (Hebrews 2:18). He is not "a high priest who is unable to sympathize with our weaknesses, but one who in every respect has been tempted as we are, yet without sinning. Let us then with confidence draw near to the throne of grace, that we may receive mercy and find grace to help in time of need" (Hebrews 4:15,16).

Notes

1. Cf. J. G. Machen, *The Virgin Birth of Christ* (New York: Harper & Brothers, 1930), 415 pp.

2. Cf. W. M. Ramsay, *Was Christ Born at Bethlehem?* (2d edition; London: Hodder and Stoughton, 1898), 280 pp.

3. Dionysius Exiguus (died c.550) established the present calendar "Anno Domini," calculating the birth to have occurred in the year 754 A.U.C. (from the founding of the city of Rome). We now know that Herod died shortly after an eclipse of the moon which occurred March 12-13, 750 A.U.C., and Jesus was born prior to that, perhaps 748 or 749 A.U.C.—6 or 5 B.C. The birthday was set at December 25 in the fourth century, without historical basis.

4. Nevertheless they do hang on, in superstition, in ecclesiastical art, and often in anti-Christian writings.

5. Elementary schools were started in Jerusalem by Rabbi Shim'on ben Shetach, c.75 B.C., but whether they had extended to Galilee by Jesus' day is not definitely known.

6. On this, and on the temptations, see particularly G. Campbell Morgan, *The Crises of the Christ* (New York: Fleming H. Revell Company, 1903), pp. 107-210.

7. One of the greatest books on this subject, in my opinion, is G. Campbell Morgan, *The Teaching of Christ* (New York: Fleming H. Revell Company, 1913), 333 pp. But, much as I value this book, having worked through it countless times, I feel it falls far short of exhausting the subject.

8. I did not say that He had *only* the same relationship. The mystery of His two natures, even though it may lie beyond our comprehension, enters at every point in His life.

9. There have been other "resurrections," in which men and women, boys and girls, have been restored to this life, as recorded in the Scriptures. But none of them knew the resurrection by which they passed beyond death into the life of the world to come.

10. The word *horisthéntos* has been variously translated, and is discussed extensively in commentaries on Romans. One thing it clearly can *not* mean is that Jesus *became* the Son of God by the resurrection; He *was eternally* the Son of God, but the great public declaration of the fact was accomplished by the resurrection.

11. See I John 2:6; Ephesians 4:1; I Peter 2:21; Galatians 5:1; John 13:15—to which could be added many others.

CHAPTER 1

John the Baptist

Jesus once said, "Among those born of women none is greater than John" (Luke 7:28). If you go through the teachings of Jesus and note particularly the things He has to say about John the Baptist, you will probably be surprised at the unusually strong statements. Yet John the Baptist is frequently overlooked. Paul and Peter and John are well known. But what do we know about the Baptist? Some men remember that he wore a camel's hair coat, and that he lost his head when a drunken king made a rash promise to a dancing girl—usually they know her name—and that is about all. That should be corrected. If Jesus placed such a high estimate on John the Baptist, we should try to learn more about him.

John the Baptist and the Old Testament.   John is

the link between the Old and New Testaments. Jesus accepted this link.

The story of the birth of John is in itself startling. "In the days of Herod, king of Judea, there was a priest named Zechariah, of the division of Abijah; and he had a wife of the daughters of Aaron, and her name was Elizabeth" (Luke 1:5). Both of them were of priestly families, devout, "walking in all the commandments and ordinances of the Lord blameless. But they had no child" (Luke 1:6,7). Perhaps in our Western society it is difficult to understand just how deeply the Semitic world felt childlessness. It was often looked on as a curse, and was considered sufficient reason in some places for a man to divorce his wife and take another. Zechariah and Elizabeth prayed about the matter.

One day, as Zechariah was fulfilling his duty in the temple (it was given to each priest to minister in the temple and light the sacred fire once in his lifetime) the aged priest had a vision. An angel said to him, "Do not be afraid, Zechariah, for your prayer is heard, and your wife Elizabeth will bear you a son, and you shall call his name John" (Luke 1:13). Notice the devotion of the father and mother! They were continuing to pray for a son, even though they were past the prime of life. Is that not what the angel's words mean, for why else would the promise of a son be connected with the words, "your prayer is heard"?

The child was to be filled with the Holy Spirit. He was to bring joy and gladness not only to the family into which he was to be born, but to other people as well. He was to "turn many of the sons of Israel to the Lord their God . . . to turn the hearts of the fathers to the children, and the disobedient to the wisdom of the just, to make ready for the Lord a people prepared" (Luke 1:16,17). All the power of inspired prophecy was to be in him, for the Holy Spirit who inspired the prophets of the Old Testament was to come upon a human being once more that he might speak the word of God. All the hopes of a brighter tomorrow that had been hidden in the hearts of these people for several centuries were to be realized because of this child that was to be born.

There was no breach with the past. God was not saying, "I am through with My people. Those Scriptures that you have been reading for generations and that religion you have been following are now abolished, and We are going to start something new." Some may present Christianity as a breach with the past, but that is not the truth. Rather, God is saying, "We are continuing the old in the new. The same spirit that came upon the prophets is going to come upon this child, and because of this fact, the people are going to be ready when I send My redeemer into the world."

Christianity does not repudiate the Old Testament. It does not say that the Bible begins with the Gospel of Matthew. Christianity says that the Scriptures of the Old and New Testaments are the Word of God. Jesus expressly said that He had not come to abolish the Old, but to fulfill it (cf. Matthew 5:17). John the Baptist rightly bridges the two; he is the prophet of the Old and the forerunner of the New.

John the Baptist and Judaism.[1] Judaism was in its formative period and at that time was a house divided. In the New Testament we hear of the Pharisees and

29

the Sadducees; there were also other factions not mentioned by name. Herod, who sat upon the throne, was an Edomite and could scarcely claim to be a Jew. The prophetic voice had been silent: the famine of the word of God had been promised by the prophet (Amos 8:11). For centuries no prophet had spoken in Israel, and in the place of prophetic religion there had settled down upon the nation a curious mixture of formalism and rationalism and separatism. Not that these were all found in the same place: that is why I called it a house divided.

There were the Pharisees, the purists, who held to the letter of the law. Jesus was critical of the Pharisees, and pointed out that they were not instrumental in the redemptive work of God in the world. They had failed to bring men to realize that God was seeking to free them; rather they were binding men to a bondage that was far more rigid than God had ever intended.

They had reduced the glorious religion of the Old Testament to a system of ritual and rites and ceremonies, to things that should be done and things that should not be done, to tithes that should be given and tithes that were not required. They had paid attention to garden herbs, and ignored the more important matters of the Law (see Matthew 23:1-36).

Then there were the Sadducees, the old conservatives. That will strike some as a strange label, but a careful study of the Sadducees will justify it. They were the dead conservatives, so dead that they repudiated any notion that had come along since the time of Moses. They were not interested in the rest of the Old Testament, and if they did not find it in the Law, they wanted nothing to do with it. They were not only the starched traditionalists, but worse, they were hardened by rationalism. Having set down the lines within which truth as they understood it must conform, they had rationalized it until there was very little spirit left, and very little place for God's Spirit to work. They had taken over the priestly caste (the priests were the sons of Zadok, or Zadokites, which is probably the derivation of the name "Sadducees") and they sought to dominate the religious life of the nation.[2]

The Jewish historian, Josephus, mentions a third sect of Judaism, namely the Essenes. As I understand this movement, it was composed of those who had rejected the dead ritual of the Pharisees, who had grown tired of the starched conservatism of the Sadducces, and who sought the answer in asceticism. The Essenes wanted to get away from the world, to live in the desert, to have no part in the Jerusalem religion but rather to have their own true religion. The famous Dead Sea Scrolls were being produced in the century or so before the birth of John the Baptist. Most scholars working on the Dead Sea Scrolls are convinced that they were written by Essenes or by those very closely allied to Essenism.[3] The Qumran literature makes it quite clear that there were Jews who looked upon the Jerusalem priesthood as wicked, who repudiated the rest of Judaism, and who formed a separatist movement.

There were other divisions in Judaism, in addition to these three, but these will suffice to make the point that Judaism was no longer a single people worshiping God in God's way, but a set of factions, filled with suspicion, distrust, and hostility, so that it was possible to throw the Sanhedrin into a turmoil just by mentioning the word "Pharisee" (cf. Acts 23:6-10).

Where does John fit into this? Well, John was apparently an ascetic, who drank no wine nor strong drink (Luke 1:15) and who was in the wilderness until "the day of his manifestation to Israel" (Luke 1:80). His food was vegetarian, or nearly so (locusts and wild honey), and his clothing was coarse (Mark 1:6). He was apparently not one of the Pharisees, and certainly not one of the Sadducees. He has often been identified as an Essene, and as often this has been denied.[4] Recently, he has been identified with the Qumran group.[5] Now, Qumran was certainly one of the few places in the wilderness of Judea capable of supporting life. John and the Qumranians both traced their origin to the priestly line. Both practised baptism. Both were ascetic. Both claimed Isaiah 40:3 as their keynote.

But on the other hand, there are important differences. The Qumran group was esoteric: only for those initiated into the group. There is nothing like this in John's preaching. The attitude of Qumran was to withdraw from the world. John, on the other hand, went back to the world to preach a message of repentance. The Qumran message was to withdraw from the world in asceticism. This certainly was not John's message. Rather, he said, in effect, "Conform your life to your faith in the world. Bring faith and life together." The soldier, asking what he should do, was not told to give up his military life; he could still be a soldier. The tax collector could still be a tax collector. The king could still be a king. But whatever he was, his service was to be rendered in accordance with the will of God. Finally, the Qumran group was waiting for a Messiah yet to come. John the Baptist was proclaiming that the Kingdom of God was present.[6]

John the Baptist and the world. One day, John left the wilderness to go to preach to the sinful world. Luke gives us the date by naming officials of the time. If you could ask the seven persons who are named what was the most important thing they had done in life, you would receive all sorts of answers; but so far as Luke was concerned, they were significant for dating the beginning of the ministry of John the Baptist: "In the fifteenth year of the reign of Tiberius Caesar, Pontius Pilate being governor of Judea, and Herod being tetrarch of Galilee, and his brother Philip tetrarch of the region of Ituraea and Trachonitis, and Lysanias tetrarch of Abilene, in the high-priesthood of Annas and Caiaphas, the word of God came to John the son of Zechariah in the wilderness" (Luke 3:1,2). It is almost as though Luke is saying, "Now I'm not sure which one of these men will be remembered, so I shall list seven and hope that one turns out to be significant." Fortunately, it is known that the fifteenth year of Tiberius Caesar was about A.D. 27 or 28. It may have been a sabbatical year; if so, that would explain why the Jews were able to go to the Jordan in great numbers to hear this prophet.

John's message is a striking one. It has three major points.

First, the Kingdom is here.[7] To the Jews, the hope of the Kingdom was no mere academic subject to be discussed in theological schools, and perhaps to be preached by fanatical preachers. It had become their very reason for existence. How long had they hoped? A thousand years? Two thousand? They had hoped for glorious deliverance when Moses led them out of Egypt, but soon they were longing for something better than the wilderness hardship and the endless manna. They had hoped for a place in the sun when they got their first king. When he failed, they hoped David would be the one. Then David's son. And then the hope seems to have turned into a vague dream. David's son—would David's son never come? And suddenly, here comes a man out of the wilderness to proclaim that the Kingdom is here!

That called for an investigation, and Jerusalem sent its representatives. "Who are you?" they asked; and he confessed, "I am not the Messiah." "Then are you Elijah?" "I am not." "Are you the prophet?" "No." "Then who are you? Let us have an answer for those who sent us." "I am the voice of one crying in the wilderness, 'Make straight the way of the Lord,' as the prophet Isaiah said" (cf. John 1:19-23).

Just a voice—but what a voice! And what a message! "The Kingdom of Heaven is at hand!" With such a message, it is only logical that the people should ask, "What shall we do?" Listen to what John tells them. He does not say, "Attend the services more regularly; give tithes more faithfully; pray more earnestly." Rather, he says, "He who has two coats, let him share with him who has none; and he who has food, let him do likewise" (Luke 3:11). If the Kingdom of God is here, it is time to begin living like members of the family of God. Tax collectors said, "What shall we do?" John did not say, "Leave your job, you puppets of Rome!" He said, "Collect no more than is appointed you." Soldiers asked him, "And what shall we do?" How many times this verse has been overlooked by well-meaning Christians who seek to force nonviolence on the world. John did not say, "Get out of the army; you cannot be a member of the Kingdom and bear arms!" No; rather, he said, "Rob no one by violence or by false accusation, and be content with your wages" (cf. Luke 3:12-14).

Perhaps King Herod asked him one day, "What must I do?" It is clear that John told him, for later Herod had a guilty conscience about John. Herod had been responsible for the imprisonment and death of John, because John had told him, "It is not lawful for you to have your brother's wife" (cf. Matthew 14:1-12).

When the Kingdom comes, it is time to set our lives in order, for the coming of the Kingdom means the coming of judgment.

The third part of John's message was, "Repent!" The word, as everyone knows, means to turn around, change your attitude. Psychologists tell us that it is impossible in certain mental conditions for a person to be helped until first he decides he wants to be helped. They can do nothing with an alcoholic until the alcoholic definitely wants to be cured. That is why one school of modern psychology puts so little emphasis on counsellor advice, and so much stress on client self-analysis and determination. First, there must be a change of attitude. Even so, before God can help us, we must repent.[8]

Repent! The things you are doing that cannot stand before judgment must go. You will have to make up your mind to do things in God's way, if you want to live in God's Kingdom. Be baptized! Let your repentance be publicly declared. Take your stand in the world for God and His Kingdom. Bring forth fruits

35

worthy of repentance! For after all, men will judge you, and not only you, but the Kingdom you represent, by your fruits.

John the Baptist and his followers.   John won many followers, and they loved him. Some of them became Jesus' first disciples (John 1:35-42), but there were others who never followed Jesus. The teacher is not always able to influence all his students. John taught his disciples to pray (Luke 11:1). He taught them to fast (Matthew 9:14). But more than religious acts, he taught them a religious attitude. They developed a tremendous loyalty, so much so that when Jesus put a question to the rulers about the source of John's baptism, they feared to answer because of the people (Matthew 21:25,26).

The ministry of John lasted possibly only six months. But twenty years later there were disciples of John the Baptist at Ephesus (Acts 19:1-7), and probably at Alexandria (Acts 18:24,25).

One wonderful day it was John's privilege to point to Jesus and say to his followers, "Behold, the Lamb of God, who takes away the sin of the world!" All his life was lived for that moment. From then on, it was, "He must increase, but I must decrease" (John 3:30).

Notes

1.   For a Jewish estimate of John the Baptist, see Josephus, *Antiquities,* 18.5.2.

2.   It is difficult to evaluate the source material on the Sadducees, since it has come down to us only through Pharisee eyes and the New Testament. But the picture is much the same in these

sources, and reasonably reliable. The new material added by a study of the Dead Sea Scrolls, in my opinion, strongly confirms this view.

3. See *Amazing Dead Sea Scrolls,* William S. LaSor (revised edition; Chicago: Moody Press, 1959), pp. 177-189.

4. For the identification, cf. K. Kohler, "Essenes," in *Jewish Encyclopaedia* (New York: Funk & Wagnalls Co., 1903), vol. 5, esp. pp. 231-232. For a thorough discussion of the opposite viewpoint, see J. B. Lightfoot, *St. Paul's Epistle to the Colossians and to Philemon* (London: Macmillan and Co., 1875), pp. 158-179.

5. Cf. Jean Steinmann, *Saint John the Baptist and the Desert Tradition* (tr. M. Boyes; New York: Harper & Brothers, 1958), 191 pp.; but see also Millar Burrows, *More Light on the Dead Sea Scrolls* (New York: Viking Press, 1958), pp. 56-63.

6. Several points here have been drawn from the very lucid discussion by Robert B. Laurin, article "John the Baptist," in *Baker's Dictionary of Theology* (Grand Rapids, Mich.: Baker Book House, 1960), p. 299.

7. For a clear discussion of the Kingdom, see George Eldon Ladd, *The Gospel of the Kingdom* (Grand Rapids, Mich.: Wm. B. Eerdmans Publishing Co., 1959), 143 pp.

8. I am aware that some will insist that man can do nothing at all, not even repent, unless God's spirit moves him. It is possible to be so logical as to be unbiblical! I am glad that when they asked John, "What shall we do?" he did not say, "Wait until the Spirit moves you to repent."

CHAPTER 2

Andrew

In a series on the great personalities of the New Testament, what shall we do about the twelve apostles? In one sense, all of them are great—great enough to have been chosen by Jesus. On the other hand, we know very little about several of them, and if we were to expand that in each case by what we know of the entire group, it would be repetitious. A few stand out with clear distinction: Peter, of course, and James and John. Is there one we can select to serve as a representative of the others? I think there is, and I have chosen Andrew for that place. Let me tell you why.

Andrew the disciple. How did Jesus begin His ministry? If you use the Gospel of Mark as a starting point (which is often used as a chronological basis for studying all the Gospels), you may get a mistaken idea that one day, when Jesus was walking along the Sea of

Galilee, He saw two men fishing, and said, "Follow me and I will make you become fishers of men" (Mark 1:17), and that was it. Now tell me, would you give up your source of livelihood and follow a stranger? Neither would I. And I do not think Simon and Andrew did.

Most scholars today agree that it is impossible to harmonize the four Gospels (i.e. edit them so as to give one continuous and chronological account). Nevertheless I would like to try. You may not agree; but this is how I see it.

John the Baptist was baptizing, and the officials were sent to investigate his credentials. In the course of the conversation, John said, "Among you stands one whom you do not know, even he who comes after me" (John 1:26,27). The next day, he saw Jesus coming toward the group he was speaking to, and he said, "Behold, the Lamb of God, who takes away the sin of the world! This is he of whom I said, 'After me comes a man who ranks before me, for he was before me'" (John 1:29,30).

This was after the baptism of Jesus, as is clear from the verses that follow (31-34). And it was after the temptations; therefore at least forty days after the baptism. Meanwhile, John had continued his baptizing and preaching, and his disciples had continued to learn from him and to assist him. Hence it follows that they had had a chance to talk with John about this Figure who had come to be baptized, and on whom the dove descended.

The next day, John was talking with two of his disciples—I gather that the crowd was not present on this occasion—and seeing Jesus, John said, " 'Behold, the Lamb of God!' The two disciples heard him say this, and they followed Jesus . . ." (John 1:35-37). One of the two was Andrew; the other is not named, but the best solution to the problem is to recognize him as John the son of Zebedee.[1] The two went with Jesus and spent the rest of the day in His presence. Andrew went and found his brother Simon and brought him to Jesus (cf. John 1:39-42).

The following day, Jesus found Philip, who may have been another of the disciples of John the Baptist; and Philip found Nathanael, much as Andrew had found Simon. It is not incredible that John found his brother James. So, within a few days Jesus had gathered about Himself five or six of His first disciples.

We have been using the word "disciples." Let us define our term before we go further. A *disciple* is one who comes under the discipline of another. The pupil is the disciple of the teacher; although this term is not generally used today when a pupil has several or many teachers. Jesus wanted these men around Him continuously, so He could teach them, by word and by deed. Only thus would they become His disciples.

Jesus had many disciples. Some of them, such as Andrew and the other who was unnamed, had been disciples of John the Baptist, and then had become disciples of Jesus. Others were added during the days of His ministry. Some became strongly attached to their teacher and His teachings. Others became impatient with His program, and turned away from Him (cf. John 6:66). Some of His disciples were trained by the method of learning-through-doing, as were the seventy disciples who were sent out two by two (Luke 10:1-20). So it is possible for us to speak of the twelve disciples,

41

the seventy disciples, or the great multitude of disciples; it is possible to speak of active disciples and passive disciples; it is possible to speak of true disciples and false disciples.

Andrew was a disciple: he was under the discipline and instruction of Jesus. It is accurate to say that he was the first disciple, or at very least one of the first two disciples. He had been a disciple of John the Baptist and was turned to Jesus by John. He had been called into discipleship by the sea in Galilee. He was in the closest circle of discipleship, and remained a faithful disciple throughout the ministry of Jesus.

Jesus not only taught the Twelve;[2] He sent them out on a preaching mission (Matthew 10:5-33). That the details expressed in verses 9 and 10 were not intended to be applied literally throughout the age is clearly indicated in the words of Jesus Himself in Luke 22:35,36.

Andrew the missionary. The distinction between "apostle" and "missionary" as used here is the difference between theory and practice. My choice of words is probably not good; but I have been unable to do better. We have seen Andrew, as a representative of the Twelve, called and trained as a disciple, appointed and given the principles of the office as an apostle. Now we want to see how Andrew carried out his mission. Have you ever thought of a missionary as simply a man or woman who is carrying out a mission?

Andrew had a mission; it was to tell people about the Lord Jesus Christ. And one of the reasons I have chosen Andrew for this study is simply because he was always finding someone and bringing him to Jesus.

The first day Andrew met Jesus, he had to tell somebody about Him. And the first person he thought of was his own brother. "One of the two who heard John speak, and followed him, was Andrew, Simon Peter's brother. He first found his brother Simon, and said to him, 'We have found the Messiah' (which means Christ). He brought him to Jesus" (John 1:40-42). There are several possible attitudes that a man can have toward his own brother. He can despise him; he can ignore him; he can want to help, but because of his approach, he offends his brother; he can have great influence over him. The most difficult relationship is the last mentioned: the man who has true love and ability to express that love in such a way as to influence his brother. Andrew was such a man. He was interested in his brother Simon. He thought first of Simon. He wanted to share his new blessing with Simon. That was good. But what a revelation it is of the relationship to read, "He brought him to Jesus"!

I wonder if Andrew also brought Philip to Jesus? It is pure speculation, I admit, but they were both from the same town (Bethsaida: John 1:44); they both had Greek names, whereas the rest of the apostles had Hebrew names; their names are often joined in the New Testament; and on two occasions Philip came to Andrew to get his help or advice on some problem. If Andrew did bring Philip to Jesus, then he was also responsible for Nathanael (John 1:45)—but that, I repeat, is speculation.

One day, at the height of Jesus' popularity, He was teaching by the sea and a large crowd had gathered. The wonderful words continued to flow, perhaps urged on by the eager assemblage, until the day was almost gone. Now, there had been no indication that the meeting would last so long, and the people were not prepared for such an eventuality. There was nothing for them to eat. Jesus asked Philip, "How are we to buy bread, so that these people may eat?" The author adds, parenthetically, that this was to test Phillip (John 6:5,6). Philip saw the financial difficulties in the problem. Andrew, who must have been near enough to overhear the conversation, had a different approach. "There is a lad here who has five barley loaves and two fish; but what are they among so many?" (John 6:9). Obviously, Andrew did not see any solution to the problem, but he did see a personal angle: he brought the boy to Jesus, and we all know the wonderful way Jesus multiplied the boy's gift to take care of the entire crowd.

Some months later, in the last week of Jesus' ministry before His atoning sacrifice, the Twelve were with Jesus in Jerusalem. And in the throngs that were there to take part in the coming feast of the Passover were some Greeks, proselytes to Judaism from the Gentile world. They wished to have an opportunity to talk with Jesus, and they found Philip, whose name probably indicates that he was a Greek-speaking Jew. Once again, Philip took the matter to Andrew, and Andrew took Philip and the request to Jesus (John 12:20-22).

The author of the Gospel does not tell us the outcome; he has used the story to move into discussion of the "hour" that had come. We suppose that Jesus acceded to the request; we know that Andrew was busy trying to bring men to the Saviour.

In the calendar of the Church of England, Saint

Andrew's Day, November 30, is the day on which it is customary to have a sermon on missions. George Milligan regards Andrew as the first home missionary, for bringing Peter to Jesus, and the first foreign missionary, for bringing the Greeks to Jesus.[3] Whether we agree with this terminology or not, I am sure we agree that in principle Andrew represents all missionaries, even as he represents the lesser known but equally important members of the apostolic band.

Notes

1. One of the strongest arguments, it seems to me, is the fact that James and John, who in the other three Gospels are part of the "inner circle" (Peter, James, and John), are not mentioned in the first twenty chapters of John. This can only be satisfactorily explained as modesty on the part of the author.

2. For a detailed study of this training, see A. B. Bruce, *The Training of the Twelve* (3d edition: New York: Richard R. Smith, Inc., 1930), 552 pp.

3. Cf. "Andrew," in Hastings' *Dictionary of Christ and the Gospels,* vol. 1, p. 53.

CHAPTER 3

Lazarus

What happens when Jesus comes into a home? Does He release the Christ-spirit that enables you to meet every difficulty with poise? Does He guarantee health and happiness and joy unbroken? Come with me inside a home where Jesus often visited, and meet some people who loved Jesus and whom He loved: the family of Martha and Mary and Lazarus.

Perhaps you are wondering what Lazarus did that he should be included in the great personalities of the New Testament. Some men enjoy reflected greatness. It is not so much what they do, as it is what happens to them, that makes them great. Because of what happened in the home of Lazarus, particularly because of what happened to him, crowds came to see him and crowds came to see Jesus. Because of what happened, crowds thronged the way into Jerusalem on the day that has come to be known as Palm Sunday. Because of the sudden surge of popularity—and so near Jerusalem, too!—the rulers decided to put Jesus to death at once. Because of the embarrassing evidence that Lazarus himself had suddenly become, the rulers decided to put him to death likewise. In the light of these momentous events, who can gainsay a place of prominence, even greatness, for Lazarus?

The home of Lazarus. There were two sisters and a brother, and the Scripture lists them in the order: Martha, Mary, and Lazarus (John 11:5). This in itself is remarkable in a world where women are usually named last, if, indeed, they are named at all. (We recall that the sisters of Jesus were not named.) The suggestion is reasonable that Lazarus was the younger brother, and Martha the oldest member of the family. According to tradition, for what it may be worth, Lazarus was thirty years old when the miracle took place, and lived thirty years more. If so, we could suppose that Martha was in her late thirties or early forties.

It is generally stated that the brother and the two sisters lived in Bethany. This village is located on the eastern side of the Mount of Olives, a little more than a mile and a half from Jerusalem, and was the starting point for the Palm Sunday procession.

Jesus was closely tied to this family in the bonds of love. We get the impression that Jesus not only visited the family, but that He felt free to drop in at any time. During the last week of His life, when He spent no night in Jerusalem, He may have made Bethany His home. His love for this family is specifically stated thrice (John 11:3,5,36) and implied throughout the story. Now let us see what happens in a home where Jesus is a frequent visitor and an intimate friend.

The home was a home of love, but it was not without its quarrels. Luke tells us about a dinner that was being prepared for Jesus, in the account of which Martha and Mary are the principal characters. The two women have the same characteristics in John's Gospel as are recorded by Luke. Martha was the fussy type; Mary was a bit carefree. When she entertained, Martha wanted everything to be just right. We all know women like her: the living room must be immaculate, the window drapes must be just so, the flowers on the table must not clash in color with the table setting; the best china and silver must be used, and everything arranged exactly right. The house is referred to as Martha's (cf. Luke 10:38). This probably refers to proprietary rights, but we get the feeling—and probably any visitor would have gotten the same impression—that Martha was running things in that house, no matter who owned it.

Mary, it seems, cared little about details. She liked a house to look "lived in," and toys on the floor or disarranged cushions on the sofa never bothered her. When they had interesting company, she would rather sit and listen than stir the soup. We are not told whether these women had been married, but if not, perhaps it was because Martha was too efficient, and Mary was too easygoing.

Martha and Mary! What happened when Jesus came into the home? Did they suddenly resolve their tensions? Did they fall into loving embrace? Did Martha stop fussing, and did Mary start spending more time in the kitchen? We know better than that. Mary sat at Jesus' feet, and Martha said to Jesus, "Don't you care that my sister has left me to do all the work? Tell her to help me!" (cf. Luke 10:40). If we could only hear the tone of voice in Jesus' answer: "Martha, Martha, you are anxious and troubled about many things; one thing is needful. Mary has chosen the good portion, which shall not be taken away from her" (Luke 10:41,42). There is a minor textual problem here, as our Bible notes in the margin. Jesus may have said, "Few things are needful" rather than "one thing." It makes little difference. If we may paraphrase, He is saying something like this: "Now, Martha, let's stop and think about life. There are really not many necessary things. You are concerned with a lot of details, but you could live without them, if you had to. On the other hand, there are a few things that you just cannot live without, and Mary has found one of these. It shall not be taken from her." Jesus does not really condemn Martha, does He? And He does not praise Mary for her indifference in the home. The point that Jesus wants to get across is simply this: there ought to be a place in the busyness of life for meditation at Jesus' feet.

The sickness and death of Lazarus. One day Lazarus became seriously ill, and they sent word to Jesus, "He whom you love is ill" (John 11:3). Then follows a very strange statement: "Now Jesus loved Martha and her sister and Lazarus. So when he heard that he was ill, he stayed two days longer in the place where he was." That little word "so" relates the sentence that follows to the sentence ahead of it, and it means that when Jesus heard of Lazarus' illness, because of His love for the family He delayed for two days before responding to the message. That is a strange kind of love, is it not? If I were to send word to a very dear friend, "I need you; come at once," and he were to reply, "I love you dearly, am leaving in two days," I would feel that our friendship was wearing thin. But think a minute! Can it be that Jesus is deliberately delaying for a reason? The teaching that God always answers prayer immediately needs rethinking.

There is another strange statement in this story: "When Jesus heard it he said, 'This illness is not unto death; it is for the glory of God . . .'" (John 11:4). Be careful how you read! The illness did result in death (John 11:14). But the purpose of the illness was that the Son of God might be glorified by means of it —that is, by means of the illness and the death.

Jesus and the disciples were beyond the Jordan when they received the news about Lazarus. The trip from Bethany to Jericho can be made in a day (it is a little over twenty miles, downhill), and Jesus was probably not far on the other side of the Jordan. The return trip is much more difficult, for starting about 1,100 feet below sea level the road climbs to nearly 2,700 feet above sea level; and to make a trip of perhaps twenty-five miles altogether, and climb 3,700 feet at the same time is a gruelling day's journey. It took, then, a day for the news of Lazarus to reach Jesus; He delayed two days; and it took at least a day for the journey to Bethany. When Jesus reached Bethany, Lazarus was already dead four days; in other words, Lazarus, as Jesus knew (John 11:14), was already dead

when the news reached Jesus. We are forced to conclude that Jesus delayed His visit, not in order to let
Lazarus die, but in order that the full impact of that
death and the resurrection that was to follow might
be felt by all who were present.

When Jesus was nearing Bethany, news of His coming preceded Him, and Martha (the active one!) went
out to meet Him. Mary sat in the house. For four
days, they had doubtless said to each other, "If Jesus
had only been here!" When Jesus came, they said it
to him, "If you had been here, my brother would not
have died" (John 11:21,32). There was no false appearance of peace and calm. Their hearts were broken.
Death means heartbreaks, even when there is faith.
To say, "If you know the truth, death will not touch
you" is sheer nonsense. To say, "There is no death;
it is only illusion" is utter folly. Death will break your
heart. It broke the hearts of Martha and Mary. It even
broke the heart of Jesus: "Jesus wept" (John 11:35).

Jesus was touched by all human infirmities. I cannot
believe that He ever looked at anyone who was ill,
deformed, or handicapped in any way, without feeling
compassion. I cannot believe that He ever looked at
a passing funeral without grieving. Yet it is a fact
beyond any contradiction that He did not cure all the
sick or raise all the dead. He had it in His power.
As a matter of fact, He had it in His power to abolish
all sickness and death, just as much at that time as
in the age to come. What we must realize is the simple
truth that it is not God's will to banish disease and
death in this present age! Until sin is removed from
God's universe, disease and death must remain. Death
is the last enemy to be destroyed. It would be no

blessing to give eternal life to men who do not know how to use it! That would be eternal hell!

But Jesus did heal some diseases and He did raise some from the dead to convince men that He has the power which He claims and which He someday plans to use on a universal scale. Lazarus is perhaps the supreme example.

Jesus said to Martha, "Your brother will rise again" (John 11:23). Martha believed in the general resurrection, but she did not dare to hope that Jesus was speaking of a special resurrection for her beloved brother. "I am the resurrection and the life," said Jesus; "he who believes in me, though he die, yet shall he live, and whoever lives and believes in me shall never die. Do you believe this?" (John 11:25,26). Martha believed that Jesus was the Messiah, the Son of God, the One who was to come into the world (John 11:27). That is splendid faith! There is not much more that anyone could believe. But it still fell short of believing what Jesus was planning to do for her. "Where have you laid him?" asked Jesus. Then, when they had come to the tomb, He said, "Take away the stone." That was too much for Martha, and she protested, "Lord, by this time there will be an odor, for he has been dead four days" (John 11:39).

Some tell us that there must be faith before there can be a miracle. Some tell us that sickness, disease, and death are not real; that if we have faith, these things disappear. Some tell us that if sickness is not healed, it is because faith is not sufficient. Read this passage over and over until you see that Martha did not have that kind of faith. If faith by itself could heal, there would be many persons alive and well today who died in faith. And if lack of faith prevented the work of God, there would be many others in misery. God asks faith—but He asks neither complete faith nor complete knowledge. He heals when and where He pleases. Some, whose faith is weak, He encourages by greater works than they would ever have believed possible. Others, whose faith is strong, He allows to drink the cup of bitter sorrow. What shall we say of the Lord Jesus Himself: was He lacking in faith? Yet He suffered and died!

The resurrection of Lazarus. After thanking God for hearing Him, Jesus cried with a loud voice, "Lazarus, come out" (John 11:43). And Lazarus came out, bound hand and feet in the grave bindings, and his face wrapped in a cloth. "Unbind him, and let him go," said Jesus—and we are reminded that Jesus did for Lazarus only what his friends could not do; He left the rest for them.

We call this "resurrection." But in a sense, it must be clearly differentiated from the resurrection to come. Jesus brought Lazarus back to this life: this life of sickness and death. There is an old tradition to the effect that when Lazarus was unbound, the first thing he said was, "Must I die again?" to which Jesus said "Yes." And from that time, Lazarus never smiled again. The tradition may not be true; but it contains a great truth. The resurrection of Lazarus was a mighty demonstration of Jesus' power over death; but it was not the resurrection unto life eternal. Only Jesus' own resurrection could demonstrate that.

The resurrection of Lazarus was of great importance for the disciples. In just a few days, their Master would be seized, tried, and put to death. Their faith would be dealt a shattering blow. He had told them, not once but several times, that it was necessary for Him to suffer, to die, and to rise again; but they were so slow to believe! Even after the experience of seeing Lazarus come out of the grave, they would have difficulty holding on to faith in Jesus. But it would help. In the years to come, when they went out into the world with the message of redemption, they might be inclined to ask themselves, "Was it all real? Did it really happen?" Then the resurrection of Lazarus would be one very important event, among many events, to reassure them.

But how would that make any difference? Simply from the whole sequence of events that the resurrection of Lazarus set off. Shortly after that event, there was a supper in Bethany, and when the news got around that Lazarus was there, a large crowd came (remember that they were very close to Jerusalem, and it was just a week before the great feast), "not only on account of Jesus but also to see Lazarus, whom he had raised from the dead" (John 12:9). The rulers had already decided, several times,[1] that Jesus would have to be put to death. The resurrection of Lazarus, however, was the climax. It was the miracle that sent Jesus to the cross. "The chief priests and the Pharisees gathered the council, and said, 'What are we to do?' . . . So from that day on they took counsel how to put him to death" (John 11:47-53). Moreover, it would be necessary to put Lazarus to death (John 12:10,11)—at least that was their plan. The day after the supper was the day of the "Triumphal Entry" into Jerusalem. While it is probably not correct to say that the crowd was there just because of the resurrection of Lazarus, still John makes it clear that there was a close connection between the two facts (John 12:18). The sequence of events may not greatly impress modern scholarship; but it would certainly have impressed those who lived through it.

The resurrection of Lazarus is a source of comfort to us also. When we are called upon to lay our loved ones in the tomb, we are in need of comfort, and it is consoling to hear the words, "I am the resurrection and the life." We need to be reminded that the Lord Jesus has the power over the grave, power demonstrated when He called Lazarus forth from the tomb. We need to be reminded, also, that death is not something foreign to the present world. It is a very real enemy that is with us and will be with us until Christ has put all enemies beneath His feet. But that day of triumph shall certainly come, just as surely as the Lord Jesus by His own resurrection became the first fruits of those who have fallen asleep (cf. I Corinthians 15:20-26).

This, then, is a home that Jesus loved, a home He graced with His presence, a home He blessed with His greatest miracle. There was no escape from the trials and tragedies of life. There was no false optimism, no unreal love. There were the normal quarrels and jealousies of any home; there were the sicknesses and anxieties; there was death and grief. The presence of Jesus in the home did not exempt that home from these things. There was faith, deep, self-committing faith, in Jesus. There was also a limit to faith, beyond which it found itself unable to go.

How much is your home like this home? The presence of Jesus in your home will not remove the realities of life, but He will help you to live through them and to triumph over them.

Notes

1. The decision is noted in John's Gospel in the seventh, eighth, tenth, and eleventh chapters.

CHAPTER 4

Peter

Peter's right to a place in the hall of fame will not be denied by anyone. In all the lists of the apostles in the New Testament he stands first. As the ready spokesman for the Twelve he assumes and is granted a place of leadership. In the first stage of the history of the Early Church he is clearly the leader, and continues to be until Paul comes into prominence.

The great challenge. One day, passing along the shore of the Sea of Galilee, Jesus saw two men at their occupation of fishing. He said to them, "Follow me and I will make you become fishers of men" (Mark 1:17). One of the two was named Simon; the other was his brother Andrew. In another place, Simon is called "bar-Jonah," which is Aramaic for "son of John." When Andrew brought his brother Simon to Jesus, "Jesus looked at him, and said, 'So you are Simon the son of John? You shall be called Cephas' (which means Peter)" (John 1:42). We should add another parenthesis, "(which means Rock)." It would be clearer if we omitted the Greek and Aramaic words, and read it simply,

"So your name is Simon? You shall be called Rock."

When Jesus called him "Rock," Simon was not very rocklike. Many times in his days of discipleship, he seemed more like shifting sand. But when we get to the end of his life, looking back over it, we are forced to admit that Jesus named him well. He was a rock. But the development of that character took time; it took experience; it took trial. Most of all, it took a basic character that had to be there in the first place. Simon had the qualities in him that Jesus needed, and Jesus had the ability to fashion Simon into what was needed for the beginning of the Church. Therefore Jesus called him Peter—Rock.

Simon, like the others of the Twelve, was first a disciple, then an apostle. He, like them, heard the call and followed Jesus. He heard, observed, and talked with Jesus. But in addition, he had the opportunity of some special training.

The great confession.   Jesus had been with His disciples for several months, possibly a year or more. The days of easy popularity and large following had turned gradually into days of stiffening opposition and hardening heart. Men who looked for a simple solution to the problems of the world were not sure that Jesus was offering the program they wanted. Ecclesiastical officials who cared more for political security than spiritual growth were afraid of the consequences of the words and works of the Galilean. Jesus had therefore chosen His Twelve, and started the intense training by which they would be ready to carry on the work when the time came. But they, too, needed sifting and testing.

One day Jesus took the Twelve away from Galilee into the region of Caesarea Philippi, located on the slopes of Mount Hermon.

Starting with a rather innocuous question, Jesus asked, "Who do men say that the Son of man is?" (Matthew 16:13).[1] That elicited interesting discussion which gives us some idea of the large and varied personality of Jesus who impressed men in so many different ways.

Jesus then asked, "But who do you say that I am?" Peter answered, "You are the Christ, the Son of the living God" (Matthew 16:15,16).

Jesus did not turn this statement aside; He accepted it. Those who deny the Messianic consciousness and claims of Jesus seem to ignore Jesus' willing acceptance of this confession of faith. "Blessed are you, Simon Bar-Jona! For flesh and blood has not revealed this to you, but my Father who is in heaven" (Matthew 16:17).[2]

Then Jesus added the words that have been discussed almost without end: "I tell you, you are Peter, and on this rock I will build my church, and the powers of death [Hades] shall not prevail against it."

It seems Jesus was designating Peter as the rock on which He was beginning the building of His Church.[3] The subsequent work of Peter in Acts will substantiate this statement.

The words that follow, "I will give you the keys of the kingdom of heaven, and whatever you bind on earth shall be bound in heaven, and whatever you loose on earth shall be loosed in heaven" (Matthew 16:19), also have to be interpreted in the light of Peter's activities in the book of Acts.

The great revelation. "From that time Jesus began to show his disciples that he must go to Jerusalem and suffer many things from the elders and chief priests and scribes, and be killed, and on the third day be raised" (Matthew 16:21). Once the issue was settled, once the apostles were committed to faith in Jesus Christ as the Son of God, Jesus undertook to prepare them for the coming passion.

Even after the great confession at Caesarea Philippi, however, Peter was not ready to accept the necessity of the ministry of suffering, and had to be strongly rebuked by Jesus (cf. Matthew 16:22,23).

Something more was needed, and in order to reveal this to His disciples, Jesus selected the three who had made the greatest progress in comprehending His revelation. We usually refer to Peter, James, and John as the "inner circle." This term is only correct if we understand that it was not a clique, it was not a steering committee or a lobby, it was not even a favored few. There was nothing of the sort in Jesus' fellowship, and when two of the three misunderstood the purpose of the special training they had been receiving, and sought for places of honor in the Kingdom, Jesus promptly set them straight.[4] Any teacher who is truly interested in his calling will devote special teaching to his more serious students. So it was that Jesus took Peter, James and John up a high mountain,[5] where He was transfigured before them (cf. Matthew 17:1-8).

The transfiguration revealed Jesus in His heavenly glory. This was Peter's evaluation, after years of considered judgment: "We were eyewitnesses of his majesty. For when he received honor and glory from God the Father and the voice was borne to him by the

Majestic Glory, 'This is my beloved Son, with whom I am well pleased,' we heard this voice borne from heaven, for we were with him on the holy mountain" (II Peter 1:16-18). Possibly this is what John referred to when he said, "We have beheld his glory, glory as of the only Son[6] from the Father" (John 1:14).

The transfiguration also set the prophecy of the coming death and resurrection against the background of the Old Testament revelation. Moses and Elijah, who appeared with the glorified Jesus on the mountain, were the representatives of the Law and the Prophets. Luke records for us the fact that Moses and Elijah "spoke of his departure, which he was to accomplish at Jerusalem" (Luke 9:31). After the resurrection, Jesus likewise emphasized the truth, that the Law and the Prophets contained all the essential elements of the passion ministry (cf. Luke 24:27, 44-47).

It was as though Jesus were anticipating questions that would be asked and objections that would be raised. One question would certainly be, "How can You be the Son of God and talk about suffering and dying?" This is a major stumbling block to many: it was to Peter, when he said, "This shall never happen to you" (Matthew 16:22); it was to many Jews, as Paul realized (see I Corinthians 1:23). So, in order that the apostles would have a clear understanding of both His mission and His person, Jesus was revealed in the effulgent glory of deity, while at the same time His death and resurrection were declared. A second question, or perhaps an objection, would be that such a ministry of suffering is not part of the Old Testament revelation of the Messiah. The presence of Moses and Elijah, and their knowledge about and interest in the sacrificial work to be accomplished at Jerusalem, anticipated that objection.[7]

The great denial. It takes human beings so long to learn! As a teacher, I am constantly on the horns of a dilemma, whether to move more rapidly to cover the subjects that need to be taught, or to move more slowly to teach the students who need to be taught. And woe to the teacher who says, "I answered that question yesterday!" or "We covered that subject last week!" Peter was slow to learn, but sometimes those who learn slowly learn best. Perhaps that is why Peter is such a helpful person to the rest of us. He learned well, when at last he grasped the lesson.

When Jesus asked, "Who do you say that I am?" Peter had the answer: "The Christ, the Son of the living God." Jesus said, "I must go to Jerusalem and be killed." Peter said, "Never!" But that is the Son of God you are talking to, Peter—you yourself just said so! When they went up to the mountain, and Jesus was transfigured before them, and Moses and Elijah were talking with Jesus about Jerusalem, Peter said, "It's nicer here; let's build three tabernacles [the word really means something like huts, lean-tos] and stay here." No wonder God spoke from heaven and said, "This is my beloved Son . . . listen to him" (Matthew 17:5)!

There was still time for Peter to learn, and in the weeks that followed Caesarea Philippi, Jesus returned to the subject of His death and resurrection more than once. Finally, the hour was at hand, and Jesus met with His Twelve for the Passover. The closing part of the ritual, which had to do with the Messianic expectation, He directed toward Himself, thereby establishing the Lord's Supper. During the meal, probably before the institution of the bread and the wine, Jesus took a basin of water, after He had laid aside His clothing and put on a towel, and He began to wash the disciples' feet. It was a needed lesson in humility and service, for the disciples had gotten so far away from the heart of the Master that they were quarrelling over greatness (see Luke 22:24-27). Peter completely missed the point of the lesson, first by protesting, "You shall never wash my feet" (John 13:8), and then by asking that he be completely washed.

Patiently, Jesus explained the meaning of His action, and said, "If I then, your Lord and Teacher, have washed your feet, you also ought to wash one another's feet" (John 13:14). Then He declared that there was a traitor in their midst—a statement that seems to have truly hit each one of the Twelve at the depths of his conscience (see Matthew 26:22). Finally, Jesus was ready to turn to the closing teaching, and He said, "Where I am going you cannot follow me now; but you shall follow afterward." Peter had a ready answer for that, "I will lay down my life for you." Then it was that Jesus told him that before the crowing of the cock at the next dawn, he would deny Him three times (see John 13:36-38).

In the garden of Gethsemane, when Jesus asked the three to watch with Him as He entered into that last great agony, they promptly fell asleep—three times! Peter was one of them (see Matthew 26:36-46). When the soldiers came to take Jesus for trial, Peter seized his sword and slashed away, hacking off the ear of the high priest's servant—as if the Son of God needed

Peter, or any other human being, to defend Him! (see Matthew 26:51-54). What was Peter trying to do? Was he trying to prevent the death of Jesus, after Jesus had tried in so many ways to show that it was necessary?.

The climax came while Peter was sitting by a fire in the courtyard of the house of Caiaphas the high priest. One of the maids saw him and thought she recognized him. "You also were with the Nazarene, Jesus." Peter denied it, and moved away. At the gateway, the maid said, "This man is one of them." Again Peter denied it. But one of the bystanders was impressed by the girl's accusation, and he noticed Peter's Galilean accent: "Certainly you are one of them for you are a Galilean." This was too much, and Peter collapsed under the strain. He not only denied knowing Jesus, but the record tells us quite clearly that He cursed and blasphemed.[8] At that moment the cock crowed, and Peter remembered the words of Jesus and broke down and wept (see Mark 14:66-72).

The great restoration. After Judas Iscariot betrayed Jesus, when he realized what he had done, he went out and hanged himself (see Matthew 27:3-10). Peter could have done the same thing. If there is any difference between Peter and Judas, it is not in the heinousness of their crime. Only our own attempts at self-justification lead us to judge Judas more harshly. To deny that you ever knew your best friend is utterly reprehensible. To deny the Lord Jesus, when you have been chosen for the express purpose of telling men about Him, is even worse. But whereas Judas went out and hanged himself, therefore denying with finality

66

that God is willing to forgive, Peter held on to some slender thread of faith.

Three days later, when women brought the incredible report that the tomb of Jesus was empty, Peter and John ran to the garden, and saw the empty grave cloths in the place where Jesus had been laid (see John 20:2-10). It seems that Peter failed to comprehend the meaning of what he saw. According to an early tradition[9] preserved by the apostle Paul (see I Corinthians 15:5), the risen Christ appeared to Peter first of the apostles. When this happened we are not told, but it must have been in the morning or early afternoon of resurrection day (cf. Luke 24:34), and it doubtless served to strengthen Peter's feeble faith. Likewise, the word of the young man to the women at the tomb, when it was reported to Peter, must have been a source of strength: "Go, tell his disciples and Peter" (Mark 16:7).

The great restoration of Peter, however, took place by the Sea of Galilee, some days later. Simon had returned to his occupation of fishing, and Thomas, Nathanael, James, John, and two others were with him. Jesus appeared on the shore and asked whether they had any fish. They had caught nothing. So Jesus said, "Cast the net on the right side of the boat, and you will find some" (John 21:6). When that resulted in a huge haul, John recognized Jesus (was it because of what had happened, rather than by sight?), and told Peter. Peter jumped into the sea, seemingly anxious to hurry to shore.

After they had eaten breakfast, Jesus turned to Peter and said, "Simon, son of John, do you love me more than these?" There was a time when Peter would have promptly said "Yes." "Though they all fall away because of you, I will never fall away" (Matthew 26:33). But now Peter will not compare himself with the others. He says simply, "Yes, Lord; you know that I love you." Jesus asked the question a second time, and a third time. Each time Peter replied in the affirmative, and each time Jesus gave him the commission to take care of His sheep.[10]

It has often been pointed out that, as Peter denied His Lord three times, Jesus gave him the chance to declare his love three times. This may well be the reason behind Jesus' threefold question. Certainly there can be no doubt that Jesus was stressing the fact that Peter was henceforth to be a shepherd of the flock of God.

Peter, a leader. According to the record in the first paragraphs of the book of Acts, the risen Jesus met with His followers from time to time during a period of forty days, teaching them about the Kingdom of God, and impressing upon them that they must wait in Jerusalem until they were baptized with the Holy Spirit (Acts 1:3-5). At the end of the forty-day period, Jesus gathered His disciples to Bethany, and, with a parting word of instruction, ascended to heaven in their sight. The disciples thereupon returned to Jerusalem, to wait in prayer for the promised Spirit (Acts 1:6-14). It was there that Peter asserted his leadership, suggesting that a successor to Judas should be chosen and setting forth the qualifications for the office (Acts 1:15-22). Matthias was chosen by lot from the two who were qualified.[11] Peter did not make the selection nor ratify it. He presided, and the disciples acted.

Peter and Jerusalem. The disciples had waited for about ten days, when suddenly on the day of Pentecost there was a sound from heaven, tongues of flame appeared on each one, and they were filled with the Holy Spirit (Acts 2:1-4). The noise must have been heard not only in the house but throughout the city, for it brought a crowd to see what was happening. When they had gathered, they were amazed by the fact that the followers of Jesus were speaking "in other tongues," and each one heard them speaking "in his own language" (Acts 2:4, 6).[12] Jerusalem was filled with pilgrims from many lands for the feast of First-fruits or Weeks—the name Pentecost had come in with Greek influence, signifying that the feast occurred fifty days after Passover—and the speaking in tongues served a twofold purpose: to startle the crowd into recognizing that a miraculous act was occurring, and to present the message in a form that would be intelligible at once to all. The miracle, incidentally, was not confined to the Twelve, but involved the entire group of disciples, about one hundred and twenty (Acts 1:15; 2:4).

After the first reaction to the miracle, the crowd became more critical, and some said mockingly, "They're drunk!" Now, much as I dislike the heckler, I am forced to admit that it is a good thing to have him around. He often speaks out the doubts that lie unspoken in the minds of others, and he keeps the speaker or doer on his toes.

Peter, standing with the other apostles, accepted the challenge and spoke to the point. They were not drunk, but this was the fulfillment of the prophecy which God had given through Joel, the outpouring of the Spirit on all flesh, to the end that whoever would call on the name of the Lord should be saved (Acts 2:17-21; cf. Joel 2:28-32). That salvation, Peter hastened to point out, was made possible by the crucifixion of Jesus Christ (Acts 2:23). It took Peter a long time to learn that lesson: from Caesarea Philippi to Calvary! But he had learned it well, and never forgot it. This crucified Jesus God raised up; this crucified and risen Jesus had poured forth the Spirit (Acts 2:22-36).

Peter's sermon applied the sword to the consciences of his hearers. If Jesus was indeed God's Anointed, and they had been responsible for His crucifixion, what should they do? Peter replied in clear terms, "Repent, and be baptized every one of you in the name of Jesus Christ for the forgiveness of your sins; and you shall receive the gift of the Holy Spirit. For the promise is to you and to your children and to all that are far off, every one whom the Lord our God calls to him" (Acts 2:38,39). This is not all that Peter said—he used "many other words"—but this is quite sufficient. It opens the door wide for all who repent to come back to God through Jesus Christ.

Peter in Judea and Samaria. The death of Stephen was the signal for the start of violent persecution and the Church was scattered throughout the region surrounding Jerusalem, that is, Judea (principally to the south and west) and Samaria (principally to the north and northwest). The apostles, however, remained in Jerusalem (see Acts 8:1-3). The scattering could be likened to scattering fire in dry brush: instead of stamping out the new faith, the persecutors only caused it to spread farther afield.

While Peter was in Joppa, a man in Caesarea, about

thirty-two miles to the north, had a vision. The man, whose name was Cornelius, was a Gentile, a centurion in the Roman army; he was moreover one of those Gentiles who had despaired of the religion of paganism, and who had found spiritual help in the religion of Israel: Cornelius was a worshiper of God. In the vision, God told him to send to Joppa, to the home of Simon the tanner, and to get Simon Peter to come to Caesarea (see Acts 10:1-8).

The next day, Peter had a vision during a noonday prayer on the rooftop. In his vision, he was being commanded to kill and eat unclean, or nonkosher food. When he refused, the voice said, "What God has cleansed, you must not call common." The vision was seen by Peter three times (Acts 10:9-16). While he was puzzling over the meaning of the vision, the emissaries of Cornelius arrived, and the Spirit told Peter, "Go down, and accompany them without hesitation; for I have sent them" (Acts 10:20).

After giving them hospitality and a night's lodging, Peter went with them to the home of Cornelius, where he told what had happened to him, and Cornelius recounted his experience. Peter began to preach the gospel of Jesus Christ, including the crucifixion and resurrection (Acts 10:39,40), but before he had finished, the Holy Spirit came on the assembled group as He had on the day of Pentecost, and the Gentiles began to speak in tongues (Acts 10:46). Peter was convinced by this miracle that God had included Gentiles in the redemptive work, and therefore he baptized those who were present (Acts 10:47,48).

News of this reached the apostles and other members of the church in Judea, and when Peter returned to

Jerusalem an inquiry was held. Peter told the story of his vision and his experience in the home of Cornelius. His closing words summarized the argument: "If then God gave the same gift to them as he gave to us when we believed in the Lord Jesus Christ, who was I that I could withstand God?" (Acts 11:17).

This incident has often been referred to in such terms as "the Gentile Pentecost," "Peter's second use of the keys," etc. In the light of Acts 15:7 it is probably correct to say that Peter used the keys of the Kingdom to open heaven's gates to Gentiles as well as to Jews. We shall safeguard our ideas against extremes if we recall that Peter did not act unilaterally: he did only what God instructed him to do, and he had to account to the apostles and the brethren for his actions.

Peter unto the ends of the earth. Herod Agrippa I had gradually acquired control of Palestine, his most recent additions being Judea and Samaria. As a Jew (which Herod the Great was not), Agrippa soon became involved in the anti-Christian hostilities, and put to death James the brother of John (Acts 12:2), and when he saw that this pleased the Jews,[13] he proceeded to arrest Peter. The apostle escaped death only by a miraculous intervention of the Lord in answer to the prayers of the Christian community, and after reporting his deliverance to the Church, he "departed and went to another place" (Acts 12:5-17).

Where did Peter go after he departed from Jerusalem? The death of Herod Agrippa I occurred in A.D. 44. According to some Roman Catholic scholars who follow the tradition preserved by the church historian Eusebius, Peter went to Rome at this time; others hold that he went to Antioch, as indicated in Galatians 2:11, and at a later date went to Rome.[14] Protestant scholars are divided on the question of whether Peter was ever in Rome, probably the majority taking the negative position.[15] The problem is certainly not an item of essential faith.

Leaving tradition out of the consideration for the moment, we know from Scripture that Peter was in Antioch (almost certainly Antioch-on-the-Orontes, or Syrian Antioch) prior to the writing of Galatians. We also know that Peter was in Jerusalem for the conference. At some date between the founding of the church in Corinth (probably A.D. 51) and the writing of First Corinthians (probably from Ephesus c. A.D. 56), Peter and his wife visited Corinth—at least this seems to be the implication of Paul's reference in I Corinthians 9:5; the statement in I Corinthians 3:6, on the other hand, makes it clear that Peter did not found the Corinthian Church. If we are not persuaded that Paul's statement implies that Peter visited Corinth, we must at least admit that it testifies to missionary activity on the part of Peter, and probably an itinerant activity rather than one that was settled in any particular place. (See I Peter 1:1.)

According to an old tradition, when fierce persecution of Christians broke out in Rome, the Church there convinced Peter that he should flee. As he was leaving the city, he met the Lord Jesus who was walking toward Rome. *"Quo vadis, Domine*—where are You going, Lord?" he asked. "I am going to Rome," answered Jesus, "to be crucified again for you." At those words, Peter returned to Rome where he was crucified, head downward, because he felt he was unworthy to die in the same fashion that His Lord died.[16] This tradition may have nothing more behind it than an early attempt to explain the words of John 21:18,19. But it seems so much like Peter that many of us are willing to accept it. Traditions can sometimes be right, you know.

Notes

1. Here the expression probably conveyed little more than the force of a personal pronoun: "Who do men say I am?"

2. That the Father had revealed it does not mean that a process of consideration and discussion had not taken place, such as I have tried to describe. God's revelations are often, perhaps most often, through historic situations; dreams and visions are, I believe, less common means of revelation.

3. Some think "rock" refers to Peter's confession of faith; but according to Acts, the confession by Peter at Caesarea Philippi was not a sufficient confession. After all, the devil himself could have subscribed to the truth of Peter's confession; there is no commitment involved.

4. See Mark 10:35-56. In Matthew 20:20-28, it was the mother of James and John who actually made the request. The lesson is the same in either case.

5. Traditionally, Mount Tabor. The setting of the story, however, makes this unlikely; I believe it was Mount Hermon.

6. Some versions, through confusion of two similar Greek words, read "the only begotten of the Father." The word translated "only" means "unique, only one of its kind," and certainly does not weaken the doctrine of the deity of Christ.

7. On the transfiguration, see G. C. Morgan, *The Crises of the Christ*, pp. 213-267, and A. M. Ramsey, *The Glory of God and the Transfiguration of Christ* (London: Longmans, Green & Co., Ltd., 1949), pp. 104-147.

8. Why so many expositors have tried to tone this down I fail to understand. The words in the Scripture are the strongest possible.

9. The use of this word does not imply that it was not true; it

had been handed down, probably by word-of-mouth, until Paul was led by the Spirit to record it; see I Corinthians 15:5.

10. Two different Greek words for "love" are used in the passage, and many scholars believe that there is a difference in the meaning of these words. I fail to find the difference, but have no strong conviction on the matter.

11. Some believe that Peter erred in this suggestion, not having received the Holy Spirit as yet, and that Paul should have been the twelfth apostle. But Paul could not meet the basic requirement, which was set forth not only by Peter but by the Lord Jesus as well (if I correctly understand Mark 3:14), namely, that these men were to be eyewitnesses not only of the risen Lord, but of His previous ministry as well. If the Christian faith was to be rooted in the historical, it had to have witnesses to all that had happened historically. Moreover, the choice was not really a *successor* to Judas (no successor to James was chosen when he was killed), but rather the selection of an *alternate* who had been in exactly the same relationship to Jesus and the eleven as Judas had been.

12. The phenomenon has been called, from the Greek term used, "Glossolalia," and has come into prominence in modern times by the emphasis of the Pentecostal movement. More recently, some of the "staid old denominations," including the Episcopalians, have received publicity through the experiments of certain ministers with Glossolalia. In the absence of any Scriptural proof that the miracle has ceased, the Church should not deny the possibility that it continues, but rather try to bring it under the sound principles of I Corinthians 14:1-19.

13. I dislike to use the term, for it is misleading. At that point in the history of the Christian Church, it was almost 100 per cent Jewish. As Luke uses the term in Acts 12:3 it refers to that segment of Judaism that was hostile to the new movement.

14. Both suggestions are noted in *A Catholic Commentary on Holy Scripture*, § 833g.

15. For a good survey of the discussion of the question, see O. Cullmann, *Peter: Disciple—Apostle—Martyr*, pp. 71-77.

16. For the full story, cf. "Acts of the Holy Apostles Peter and Paul," *The Ante-Nicene Fathers*, vol. 8, pp. 844-845.

75

CHAPTER 5

Stephen

Stephen is known as the first martyr of the Christian church. He was also one of the first deacons. Stephen was chosen to take care of the temporal problems of the Church in Palestine. Nothing is said of how he fulfilled his office; but it is taken for granted he did a fine job. We are told, however, quite a lot about other work that he did, "over and beyond his call to duty." Perhaps that is not the way we should say it. These are the things that he did as a Christian, and in addition to these things he fulfilled the office of deacon. He was a "witness." All Christians have been called to be witnesses. "You shall be my witnesses," said Jesus, and the book of Acts tells the story of some of the witnesses. The duty of a witness is to tell what he knows, "the truth, the whole truth, and nothing but the truth."

Stephen was not only a witness, he was also an advocate. He was not content merely to tell what he knew, but he got into active discussion with those who did not agree with him. "Some of those who belong to the synagogue of the Freedmen (as it was called), and of the Cyrenians, and of the Alexandrians, and of those from Cilicia and Asia, arose and disputed with Stephen" (Acts 6:9). The "Freedmen"[1] were those who had been taken captive (perhaps by Pompey) and later they or their children had been set free. Cyrenians and Alexandrians came from Africa; Cilicia and (proconsular) Asia were in Asia Minor. All of the Freedmen were Hellenists.

What was it Stephen said that stirred them so deeply? Stephen was a Hellenist; how had he irritated these other Hellenists? We are not told in so many words, but I think we can reconstruct it from the story. They charged Stephen, for example, with speaking "blasphemous words against Moses and God," and "against this holy place and the law" (Acts 6:11,13). It seems obvious that Stephen had attacked the Temple (God) and the Law (Moses).[2] How? Where did he get such an idea?

If we study the teachings of Jesus, we soon discover where Stephen got his peculiar notions. Jesus denied the hereditary view of religion that said: Because our father is Abraham, we are God's children. Jesus said: In order to be Abraham's children, you must have the vital faith that Abraham had (cf. John 8:39). Jesus denied the legalistic view of the Law. The Pharisees asked, "Why don't your disciples wash their hands before eating?" (cf. Mark 7:1-5). They were referring, of course, to ritual washing, and not to sanitation. The

78

disciples might have just washed their hands; but if it had not been done according to the correct ritual, they would still be "unclean." Jesus went on to point out that "there is nothing outside a man which by going into him can defile him; but the things which come out of a man are what defile him" (Mark 7:15). Jesus challenged the righteousness of the Pharisees (see Matthew 5:20). Jesus particularly and pointedly challenged their attitude toward the Sabbath, stating as a principle that "the sabbath was made for man, not man for the sabbath" (Mark 2:27). To illustrate this principle, Jesus on several occasions deliberately broke the Sabbath (as interpreted by the traditions of the elders).[3] For example, one day in the home of a ruler of the Pharisees there was a man who had dropsy. Jesus had been invited there to dine, and it was the Sabbath. Jesus asked, "Is it lawful to heal on the sabbath, or not?" (Luke 14:3). According to their tradition, healing was work, and work was forbidden by the Sabbath commandment. Jesus deliberately forced the problem into the open, and then proceeded to heal the man.

Further, Jesus denied the view that worship was either limited to a particular place, or more advantageous if performed at a certain place. When the woman of Samaria raised the question by saying, "Our fathers worshipped on this mountain; and you say that in Jerusalem is the place where men ought to worship," Jesus replied, "The hour is coming when neither on this mountain nor in Jerusalem will you worship the Father . . . the true worshipers will worship the Father in spirit and truth . . ." (cf. John 4:20-24).

According to tradition, Stephen had been one of

the Seventy. If we prefer not to accept that tradition, we must still admit that Stephen had been taught by men who had been with Jesus. Stephen had begun to think, and the more he thought the more he realized the implications of Jesus' teachings. Law was a matter of the spirit and intent of the heart, and not mere ritual. Worship was a matter of spirit and truth, not geography. If we carry these principles to their logical conclusion, the Law can be replaced by the Spirit of God in the heart, and the Temple can be replaced by spiritual fellowship between redeemed man and his Saviour God.

To the Jew, brought up as he had been to think of the Law and the Temple as essential elements in his religion, this was a hard teaching. The Jewish Church in Acts had much difficulty at this point, and for many years the Church seemed about to be torn into two churches. Peter got into the struggle; so did James the Lord's brother, and Paul. We shall have to return to it again. For the present we simply wish to point out that Stephen was the first man to step out in faith into the deeper significance of the teachings of Jesus. And just as Jesus had run into serious difficulty and opposition, so did Stephen.

Stephen's defense. The accusation of blasphemy was serious enough to warrant a formal trial. Witnesses—false witnesses—were brought in (cf. Acts 6:13), as had been done in the trial of Jesus. When they had finished, Stephen was given the opportunity of speaking on his own behalf. The seventh chapter of Acts is usually referred to as "Stephen's defense."

It is strictly speaking not a defense of Stephen so

much as it is a defense of his teaching. He is defending Christianity. He is defending the larger view presented by Jesus. It might better be termed an "apology," using the word in the original meaning, the defense of a cause or doctrine.[4] Stephen does not mention himself. He does not mention the charges made against him. He stays with the central issue, which could be paraphrased: The prophetic view of Scripture versus the legalistic.

Let me make clear what I mean by the terms. The prophetic view of Scripture tries to get the truth out of Scripture; the legalistic view tries to force Scripture into a mold. The prophetic view says: God has spoken, now let us try to get the fullest and clearest possible meaning of what He said. The legalistic view says, God has spoken, and this is the way our fathers understood Him; this is therefore what God meant, and we shall resist any attempt to make it mean anything else.

There are many sincere people teaching the Bible today who follow in the tradition of legalism. If you were to suggest to them that they walk in the steps of the Pharisees, they would doubtless feel insulted. Yet it is quite obvious that they are not trying to let the Scripture lead them into all truth; rather, they are trying to jam the truth into the little molds which they received from those who taught them. "It was good enough for Mother, and it's good enough for me." They do not think that way of their washboard, their horse-and-buggy, or their medical doctor, but they do think it about their religion. Now it certainly must be obvious, in the light of what I have already said, that I am not challenging the fundamental doctrines of the Scriptures; I am speaking about interpretation of the Scriptures, about the application of the truth of God to the life of man.

Stephen undertook to meet the legalistic attitude by a long, involved argument. He started by pointing out that the original covenant was made by God long before the time of Moses, long before the time of Solomon; it was made with Abraham, when there was no Law and no Temple. Yet Abraham could worship God acceptably. This covenant was not made in the land of Canaan; it was made in Mesopotamia. The Law was not given in Jerusalem; it was given in Sinai. God's activity therefore had not been limited to Palestine. It had been operative on behalf of Joseph in Egypt, and again in Egypt for all of Israel. Now, if worship was acceptable to God and God's redemptive activity was available to men, before there was a Law and before there was a Temple, these things were not essential elements, certainly not essential forms. Moreover, God's revelation has been progressive. God has been dealing with the race as a parent deals with a child: a little at a time, increasing as the child increases in understanding. God's revelation increased as we pass from Abraham to Moses, and continued to increase as we pass from Moses to Solomon, and then to the prophets. Why, then, could it not continue to increase still more as we come down to the time of Jesus? If God's promise originally made to Abraham had included the blessing of the Gentiles, certainly it was not intended to stop with the Jewish people.

Now, I grant that Stephen did not say these things as I have said them. But check over his speech, and see whether I have misrepresented his train of thought.

When he came to the matter of progressive revelation, he introduced the other side: human inertia. The great problem has not been that men have moved ahead of the prophets; the great problem has been that men have refused to move with the prophets. "Which of the prophets did not your fathers persecute?" (Acts 7:52). These prophets, who had announced the coming of the Righteous One, Stephen ties in with Jesus, and the Righteous One, the Messiah of Israel, he identifies with Jesus.

This was too much! A speech like this may make its point with thoughtful men, as they have time to sit down and ponder its subsurface truth. But the mention of the murder of Jesus was inflammatory, and men of inflamed passions do not take time to sit down and think. Stephen's defense is one of the great prophetic messages of the Early Church. It is a pioneer speech that moves out into unexplored territory of thought. But its immediate result was the death of Stephen.

The stoning of Stephen. Stephen was stoned for blasphemy. According to the Law, "He who blasphemes the name of the Lord shall be put to death; all the congregation shall stone him" (Leviticus 24:16). Stephen was stoned outside the city, in accordance with the Law, "Bring out of the camp him who cursed" (Leviticus 24:14). The witnesses stoned him first, for the Law said, "The hand of the witnesses shall be first against him to put him to death, and afterward the hand of all the people" (Deuteronomy 17:7).

Not only was the Law specific on the matter, but the tradition of the Fathers was clear and detailed. The Talmud says that after the witnesses have been heard, and sentence is pronounced, the condemned man "is led forth, while some one precedes him announcing: Such a one, son of so and so, is led forth to be stoned for such an offense; so and so are the witnesses; whoever has anything to produce in his favor, let him produce it." When they are about six feet from the place of execution, the condemned man is stripped, and "one of the witnesses casts a stone, and if this does not kill the man, then another, and then, if death has not ensued, the people take up the task" (*Sanhedrin*, 6).

"One of the witnesses casts a stone, and if this does not kill the man . . ."—think of that a moment! That stone was thrown so as to kill! I have seen an angry mob take up stones. I have seen stones fly. Once I thought we were going to get stoned, but we were able to get to a waiting car. Those stones come in with the force and accuracy of big-league pitching! In such a manner Stephen was stoned to death, and like his Lord, he died uttering the words, "Lord Jesus, receive my spirit. Lord, do not hold this sin against them" (Acts 7:59, 60; cf. Luke 23:46,34).

"And the witnesses laid down their garments at the feet of a young man named Saul" (Acts 7:58). "And Saul was consenting to his death" (Acts 8:1). Augustine observed, *Si Stephanus non orasset, ecclesia Paulum non habuisset*, "If Stephen had not prayed, the Church would not have had Paul."

So Stephen, whose name means "crown," received the crown of the martyr. And so the language received another word, for the Greek word *martys* (genitive, *martyros*) originally meant simply "witness," but because of the great crowd of witnesses who paid for their testimony with their blood, came to mean what our English word "martyr" means. Stephen is the protomartyr, the first Christian martyr.

> The martyr first, whose eagle eye
>   Could pierce beyond the grave,
> Who saw his Master in the sky,
>   And called on Him to save;
> Like Him, with pardon on his tongue,
>   In midst of mortal pain,
> He prayed for them that did the wrong:
>   Who follows in his train?

Notes

1. King James Version reads "Libertines," a translation which should be rejected, since the word has come to have an immoral connotation.

2. The identification of the Temple with God may seem farfetched, but as a matter of fact, the words became so closely identified that God is still called *ha-Maqóm* ("the Place") by Jews who seek to avoid using the word for God.

3. For a forceful study of the way Jesus dealt with the Sabbath, see A. G. Hebert, *The Throne of David* (London: Faber and Faber, 1951), pp. 143-163.

4. It is an interesting illustration of the way words change in meaning, that "apology," which formerly meant, "these are the reasons why I am right," now means, "I am sorry that I made a mistake."

CHAPTER 6

Paul

In the New Testament there are two men; the one is the persecutor of the Church, the other is the apostle of Christ. The former, if he had not been crucified with Christ, would have done his best to destroy utterly the infant Church. The other, if he had not been born from above, would not only have failed to see the Kingdom of Heaven himself—you and I probably would not have seen it either. And yet, as any student of the New Testament knows, these two men are one. The first is Saul of Tarsus; the second is Paul the apostle.

Tarsus.[1] Tarsus had a long and rich history. Excavations have uncovered successive civilizations from c.4000 B.C. Situated in a rich plain, protected from the cold winter winds by the lofty Taurus mountains to the north, the region was an ideal place for a young civilization to get started. The Cydnus River, navigable as far as Tarsus for small boats, formerly emptied into the Rhegma a few miles south of the city, the Rhegma being a lake or harbor that served as a seaport for the Mediterranean. Two great trade routes passed through Tarsus, one from the Euphrates valley and the other from Egypt via Palestine and Syria; from Tarsus they proceeded first northward, to pass through the Cilician Gates (a natural pass, widened c.1000 B.C., through the Taurus range) thence to central Anatolia and the west. It is therefore no mere figure of speech to say that Tarsus was a meeting place of East and West, for commercial and military expeditions of scores of centuries passed through that city.

Antiochus IV (Epiphanes) visited Tarsus in 170 B.C. and made it an autonomous Greek city, probably planting a Jewish colony there at that time. It was made a free city by Mark Antony, and the privileges of a free city were confirmed by Augustus. To be able to claim to be a citizen of Tarsus was to claim proudly to be a citizen of "no mean city" (Acts 21:39).

Tarsus was a university city. Ramsay said it was one of the three great university cities of the Mediterranean world, but later modified that statement.[2] The two outstanding universities, it would seem from Strabo, were at Athens and Alexandria, but what Tarsus lacked in greatness, however, it made up for in zeal for knowledge.[3] The term "university" as used here does not mean what it probably implies to us today. It was not an institution with a faculty, curriculum, and student body. Rather, it was a place where lecturers who were passing through could give their lectures, where teachers could establish themselves, gathering around them townspeople and receiving from them fees by which they supported themselves. When we are discussing Saul's education, however, it is necessary for us to be reminded that there is no means of measuring the effect of this intellectual environment on Saul during his formative years.[4] He spoke Greek, the language of the city, and as Deissmann has pointed out,[5] it was the vernacular rather than the classical language of the rhetoricians. Saul was certainly acquainted with either the teachers or the writings of the Stoic school of philosophy.[6] His few quotations from the Greek poets, however, are very slender grounds on which to build a supposition of vast formal learning.[7] Tarsus was a prominent Roman city,[8] and since Saul had been born to a Roman citizen, he could claim that he was a freeborn Roman citizen (Acts 22:28). The pride and the responsibility of his citizenship became, after his conversion, an ideal worthy of the gospel, and we find it expressed several times in his writings and speeches (cf. Philippians 1:27 and Acts 23:1; see also Ephesians 2:12; and Philippians 3:20).

Far more important, however, than the Greek or Roman heritage which was Saul's in Tarsus was the heritage which was his through his parents. Both father and mother were Hebrews (Philippians 3:5), hence Saul grew up to know the God and the Scriptures of the Jewish people, even though it was in the Hellenistic world.[9] Since his father was of the tribe of Benjamin, the young boy had been named after the first king of Israel, the Benjamite Saul. His upbringing had been according to the strictest sect of the Pharisees, doubtless antedating his formal training in Jerusalem, in a home where the Law was rigidly observed. The origin of Saul's second name (Paul) is disputed; some hold that it was probably derived from the well-known Pauli family in Rome, his father having been a liberated slave who received his name and citizenship for some great service; others hold that it was taken by Saul in honor of Sergius Paulus, the proconsul whom he converted at Paphos (Acts 13:7).

So we see that Saul obtained from Tarsus the three elements so prominent in his life, and so important in the world of his day: Roman citizenship, the language and culture of Hellenism, and the religion of the Jews.

Jerusalem. Saul had a sister, and from the fact that her son lived in Jerusalem and had access to the barracks (see Acts 23:16), it is usually assumed that she lived in Jerusalem. It is further assumed that Saul went to live with this sister, probably not long after his twelfth year, becoming subsequently a disciple of the famous rabbi Gamaliel (see Acts 22:3).

This Gamaliel, known as "the elder" to distinguish him from two others of the same name, was the son of Simon and the grandson of Hillel. So highly was Gamaliel the elder regarded by the Jews that it is recorded in the Mishnah that "with the death of Gamaliel, the reverence for the law ceased and purity and abstinence died away." He was the first of seven rabbis to be called by the highest title "rabban." He was of the school of Hillel, as opposed to that of Shammai, and therefore represented a broader and more liberal view among the Pharisees (cf. Acts 5:38,39). He was interested in Greek literature, and encouraged the reading of it. He also held a more spiritual view of the Law, and encouraged Jews to have friendships and social relationships with foreigners. At the same time, there can be no doubt that he was a strict Pharisee, and that the young Saul was given training in the tenets of this sect at the feet of the great rabbi (cf. Acts 22:3).

Saul was born about the beginning of the Christian era and probably came under the influence of Gamaliel sometime in the second decade of the first century (possibly A.D. 15). The conversion of Saul is usually dated between A.D. 33 and 36, and since Gamaliel did not die until c.57 or 58, it is a reasonable assumption that Saul was under the influence of Gamaliel for several years at a time when the young disciple was at a very impressionable age, and the master in the ascendancy of a very brilliant career.

If Saul was in Jerusalem between the years A.D. 26 and 30 the question naturally comes up, had he seen or heard Jesus? Scholars can be found on both sides of the question, and quotations of Scripture can be found to support either side. Speaking for myself, I get the general impression from reading Paul's letters that he had not known Jesus prior to the resurrection.

Saul became extremely active in his zealous endeavor to keep the Law of Moses, and gained sufficient reputation that he could refer to this as proof of his earnest devotion to Judaism (Acts 22:3; 26:5).

It is not clear that Saul had engaged in the persecution of the Church prior to the stoning of Stephen. Saul was present at that event, and consented to it (cf. Acts 7:58; 8:1). This is not quite the same, however, as what he says concerning his active persecution of the Church, "I cast my vote against them" (Acts 26:10).

We might be justified in concluding that Saul was merely consenting inwardly to what was being done in the case of Stephen, and that at some later date he became a member of the Sanhedrin that took part in voting to persecute Christians unto death.[10]

Something of Saul's struggle with the demands of the Law seems to be preserved for us in the seventh chapter of his epistle to the Romans.[11] He was not finding in the Law the peace of heart that he sought, and, like Martin Luther, he had a deep struggle of soul for something which the Law could never provide. It is the nature of Law not to provide, but to demand. Law requires rigid obedience and it can neither tolerate short measures and partial fulfillment, nor provide satisfaction or forgiveness. The Law was driving Saul more and more in a relentless pursuit of something that would satisfy the deep yearnings of the heart, but it was not providing satisfaction for those yearnings. Saul's outburst of fanatical zeal against the Christian Church may be looked upon as one of the means by which he sought to satisfy the Law's demands.

In Jerusalem, "Saul laid waste the church" (Acts 8:3). The persecution was thorough and the results are reflected in Acts at several points. Saul was not satisfied, but "still breathing threats and murder against the disciples of the Lord, went to the high priest and asked him for letters to the synagogues at Damascus, so that if he found any belonging to the Way, men or women, he might bring them bound to Jerusalem" (Acts 9:1,2).

It was on the road to Damascus, for the purpose of carrying out this project, that Saul had his great experience. Luke, who has demonstrated in many ways that he is a careful author and historian, felt it necessary to record this story at three different points in the book of Acts (Acts 9:3-18; 22:6-16; 26:12-18). The accounts are sufficiently different that anyone looking for difficulties can find them; the accounts agree, however, in reporting the essential event. It was about the noon hour in the full strength of the sun, not far from Damascus, that Saul saw a brilliant light from heaven and fell to the ground blinded by it. He heard a voice saying to him, "Saul, Saul, why do you persecute me?" He replied, "Who are you, Lord?" The voice from heaven said, "I am Jesus, whom you are persecuting; but rise and enter the city, and you will be told what you are to do" (cf. Acts 9:4-6).

Damascus. At Damascus there was a disciple named Ananias, and the Lord said to him in a vision, "Rise and go to the street called Straight, and inquire in the house of Judas for a man of Tarsus named Saul; for behold, he is praying, and he has seen a man named Ananias come in and lay his hands on him so that he might regain his sight" (Acts 9:11,12). If you were Ananias, what would you do? Nothing has been said to indicate that Saul has been converted. Ananias knew, probably by the grapevine,[12] that Saul had come to Damascus to do to the Church there what he had done in Jerusalem. So Ananias began to make excuses. The Lord said, "Go, for he is a chosen instrument of mine to carry my name before the Gentiles and kings and the sons of Israel . . ." (Acts 9:15). Ananias went. As a result, Saul received his sight and was baptized (Acts 9:18). In the synagogues, Saul declared his faith, saying of Jesus, "He is the Son of God" (Acts 9:20).

Saul's hatred of Christ and the Church, if we have analyzed it correctly, was due to Saul's conviction that Jesus was blaspheming in making the claims He made, while the Christians were guilty first of failing to repudiate His blasphemy, and then of making equally blasphemous statements. This, then, is the key to Saul's new message. Jesus was either a blasphemer or He was the Son of God. Formerly, Saul had taken the view that Jesus was a blasphemer; after his conversion experience, Saul declared that Jesus was the Son of God. It is either the one or the other; there is no third position.

What made the difference? Saul makes it clear: he saw the risen Christ. If Jesus was alive, then God had raised Him from the dead. Certainly God would not raise up a blasphemer. By raising Jesus from the dead, God had declared Him to be the Son of God. It was as simple as that! Saul's statements concerning the origin of his faith leave no doubt that it did not come from the apostles; it came from his training in the Old Testament Scriptures and his personal experience of the risen Christ.[13]

After being driven from Damascus, Saul began preaching in the synagogues of the Hellenists in Jerusalem (Acts 9:29)—taking up the work, it would seem, that had been left by Stephen. Saul, of course, encountered the same opposition that Stephen had; the opposition turned to murderous hatred, and they sought to kill him. He was saved by the activity of the Christians in Jerusalem—what complete reversal of poetic justice!—and went to Caesarea, thence to Tarsus. But no longer was he the old Saul of Tarsus; now he was a new creation in Christ Jesus.

The cities of Galatia. Paul's "first missionary journey" covered the island of Cyprus and the southern portion of the Anatolian Plateau. The cities of Anatolia, after leaving the coastal region of Perga, were Antioch in Pisidia, Iconium, Lystra, and Derbe. To study these places on a map, or even to read about them in a modern guide, may leave you puzzled, for only Iconium (modern Konya) is of any importance. But a visit to Antioch (just outside modern Yalvach) will quickly convince you that this was an important and large city in the Roman period. Lystra was reasonably large. In fact, of all the cities of Paul, Derbe is the only place that was not of sizeable importance.[14]

Antioch, Lystra, and Iconium were located in the area of Galatia, and Derbe was on its southern border.[15] Paul's letter to the Galatians was written to the churches in these cities, probably to the Church at Antioch in particular, and his first recorded sermon was delivered in Antioch. The apostle had first visited Galatia as the result of some sickness, perhaps malaria contracted in the Pamphylian plain.[16] The Galatians had received him with undue kindness—they would have plucked out their eyes for him (cf. Galatians 4:15)—and Paul was bound by a strong bond of affection to them. Their later defection from the faith disturbed him emotionally, as is evident from the language of his letter to them, and this again gives us some idea of the relationship between the missionary and the people he was serving.

His sermon in Pisidian Antioch gives us several indications of his method and approach. The area was, of course, Gentile, but Paul had gone to the Jewish community and had taken his place as a worshiper in the synagogue. I suppose that Paul wore the robe of a rabbi or some indication that he was a qualified teacher in Israel—although it is possible that this information had been given upon his arrival in the city. At any rate after the reading of selections from the Law and the Prophets, the visitors were invited to speak a word of exhortation, and Paul accepted. He began with a historic survey of Israel which led through the Davidic kingship to Jesus the promised Saviour. He told of the death of Jesus at the hands of the Jewish rulers. He proclaimed the resurrection and the post-resurrection appearances of Jesus, and declared that this was the fulfillment of God's promises to the fathers. "Let it be known to you therefore, brethren, that through this man forgiveness of sins is proclaimed to you, and by him every one that believes is freed from everything from which you could not be freed by the law of Moses" (see Acts 13:14-41).

There were present in the synagogue when Paul spoke a number of Gentile proselytes ("you that fear God" in 13:16). To me one of the most discouraging features of Judaism for a proselyte would be the legalistic obligations; and some Jews would agree with me. Some have expressed themselves as not in favor of seeking to convert Gentiles in words like these, "Why make him exchange the seven commandments of Noah for the 613 commandments of Moses?" Jesus suggested that the Pharisees made it onerous for proselytes (Matthew 23:15). Imagine the reaction, then, when Paul stated that Jesus had freed all that believe in Him from the Law (Acts 13:39)! "The next sabbath almost the whole city gathered together to hear the word of God" (Acts 13:44).

In the multitude that gathered were many Gentiles, and the sight of Gentiles (not Gentile proselytes, who were acceptable) stirred up deep resentment among the Jews (Acts 13:45). This led to the great decision on the part of Paul: "It was necessary that the word of God should be spoken first to you. Since you thrust it from you, and judge yourselves unworthy of eternal life, behold, we turn to the Gentiles" (Acts 13:46).

If I understand Acts correctly, Luke has introduced this statement because it signals the beginning of a deliberate program to win Gentiles. Prior to this, if God wanted a Cornelius in the Church, there was no objection (there was a mild protest, but it was satisfactorily answered). If a few Gentiles here and there heard the message and were converted, there would be problems, but there was no overt objection. But there was no definite program to bring Gentiles into the Church. In other words, it was a Jewish-Christian Church. Paul is now launching out on a program that may make it a Gentile-Christian Church. Up to this point, the members of the Church, except for a small Gentile minority, continued to perform the ritual of Judaism. With the admission of large numbers of Gentiles, it will be only the small Jewish minority that will continue the practices of Judaism. The Gentiles "were glad" (Acts 13:48), but not the Jews.

Obviously this introduced a new problem in the young Church. When Paul and Barnabas returned to Syrian Antioch from their first journey, and told of their successes in this new Gentile campaign (Acts 14:27), they soon began to encounter opposition. Men from Judea had come and were saying, "Unless you are circumcised according to the custom of Moses, you cannot be saved" (Acts 15:1). Paul and Barnabas stubbornly rejected this doctrine, and the result was the appointing of a commission to go to Jerusalem to lay the problem before the apostles and presbyters (Acts 15:2).

This opens what is known as the Judaizer controversy, which continued in the Church for years, and its subcurrents are felt even down to the present time. The issue, bluntly stated, is simply this: *Must a Gentile become a Jew in order to become a Christian?*

We are amused by the question today. That is because we are a Gentile Church. But turn the question around: Must a Jew become a Gentile in order to become a Christian? Must an Oriental become a Westerner in order to become a Christian? Must a Negro become a white man in order to become a Christian? Basically, the question is one of second-class citizens in the Kingdom of God. Shall there be in the Church of Christ two groups: those who are saved and in addition they also keep the Law; and those inferior ones who are merely saved? Shall we erect a partition down the middle of the Church and put signs over the doors, admitting the special class members to the one side and relegating the second-class members to the other?

It makes no difference what the "plus" is, the result will be the same. The church that establishes as a rule of membership, "In order to belong to this church, you must believe in the Lord Jesus Christ and——," regardless of what is written in the blank, comes under the Judaizer problem.

At the Jerusalem conference, the Judaizers, in reply to the report of Paul and Barnabas, stated their principle: "It is necessary to circumcise them, and to charge them to keep the law of Moses" (Acts 15:5). This was debated. Peter spoke, telling of the experience he had in the case of Cornelius, and asserting his principle, "We believe that we [Jews] shall be saved through the grace of the Lord Jesus, just as they [Gentiles] will" (Acts 15:11). Barnabas and Paul were given a chance to speak. Then James the brother of Jesus, sometimes known as the Bishop of Jerusalem, summarized the problem, and gave his judgment (Acts 15:19, 20). The Church gave its answer, and appointed representatives to take that answer back to the Gentiles in Antioch of Syria. The answer: Gentiles are not to be forced to become Jews in order to become Christians! (see Acts 15:28,29). There shall be no second-class citizens in the Kingdom of God.

The cities of Greece. Paul's new program carried him farther and farther into the Gentile world on his "second missionary journey," until he had crossed over into Europe and journeyed through Greece (Macedonia and Achaia) to Athens and Corinth. These two cities symbolize the best and the worst of the pagan world. We have seen Paul as the champion of the liberty of the gospel. Now let us see how he measures up to the problems of paganism.

Athens was in many respects the glory of Greece. Architecture, sculpture, philosophy: to say these words is to think of Athens. Standing in the Agora, proclaiming Jesus and the resurrection, Paul was looking up at the Acropolis crowned by the Parthenon. Around him were the magnificent temples and statues that today, except for the Hephaesteion, are only foundations and broken bits of marble. That is where Plato had his academy, Aristotle the lyceum, and Zeno his stoa or porch. Paul mentioned none of the wonders of the city or its history; he preached Jesus and the resurrection.[17] The council of learned men, the Areopagus, wanted to know more about this doctrine, and Paul made his address.[18]

Some mocked. Some wanted to hear more—but "later." But "some men joined him and believed" (Acts 17:34). We are told that Paul failed; nothing happened, no church was founded, no epistles were written to Athens. But since when is the success of a preacher to be measured by the number of converts? If Paul had had only one convert in Athens, that one being Dionysius the Areopagite—which is the equivalent of invading a great university center and converting one of the intellectual leaders—his mission could not be called a failure. Far more important than numbers are key persons. If the Christian Church would stop measuring growth by numbers and set its sights on the political and intellectual leadership of the world, the influence of the gospel would be far greater—and the numbers would also increase.

If Athens was the glory of Greece, Corinth was its cesspool. Located on the trade routes, where ships from the west docked to transfer cargo to ships for the east (or, for smaller boats, to be rolled across the isthmus), Corinth was a typical liberty port. No, not quite typical, for on Acrocorinth, the hill behind the city, there was a temple of love with free prostitutes in great numbers for all who would worship the goddess of love. Look up the word "Corinthianize" in your English dictionary, and you will get a good idea of what

Corinth was like. In Greek, the word is even more expressive of its sin.

The Church at Corinth was made up of men and women who had for the large part been rescued from sin. Read the letters of Paul to the Corinthians, and you will quickly learn that while the Corinthians had been taken from sin, not all sin had been taken from the Corinthians. No other church in the New Testment had the problems of immorality that we find in the Church of Corinth.

Would the gospel of Jesus Christ meet the needs of the people in Corinth? Paul went there "in weakness and in much fear and trembling" (I Corinthians 2:3), but the Lord told him that He had many people there and Paul stayed a year and a half (Acts 18:9-11). I am sure that Paul soon lost his fear and trembling as he saw the power of the gospel at work in the lives of men and women redeemed from sin. The epistle to the Romans was written from Corinth on Paul's second (or third?) visit to that wicked city, and it is almost certain that Paul's picture of the sin of the Gentile world (Romans 1:18-32) was drawn from experiences such as he had in Corinth, as was his firm conviction that the gospel is the power of God for salvation to everyone that believes (Romans 1:16).

The churches in Asia. On his "second missionary journey," Paul had wanted to go into Asia, but was forbidden by the Spirit (Acts 16:6). "Asia" is used in Acts for the Roman province, and denotes a portion of southeastern Asia Minor. The principal city was Ephesus, an important seaport (although its importance in that respect was diminishing, due to the fact that the harbor was silting up), capital of the province, and terminus of the road that stretched across Asia Minor to the east, connecting with Syria, Palestine, and Egypt, with Mesopotamia, and with Persia and India. Paul not only visited Ephesus on his "third missionary journey," but even located here for an extended period possibly as much as three years (Acts 19:8,10,22).

As was customary, Paul began his work in the synagogue. Even though he had turned to the Gentiles years before (Pisidian Antioch was visited first c. A.D. 47; the Ephesian ministry began c.54), he never turned from the Jews. They were his brethren, his kinsmen, for whose conversion he could wish himself "accursed and cut off from Christ" (Romans 9:3). His invariable plan was to go to the synagogue and preach there as long as possible; at Ephesus this was about three months (Acts 19:8). Then, when that door was closed to him, he opened a school nearby (at Corinth it was next door to the synagogue, Acts 18:7), taking his disciples with him.

His daily program was to teach his disciples for some period of the day, and to visit from house to house. At Ephesus he taught in the hall of Tyrannus, according to some ancient manuscripts of Acts between the hours of 11 A.M. and 4 P.M. (Acts 19:9). Some have pointed out that this is the least likely time of the day for a school; on the other hand, as visitors to the Near East know, shops are shut during these hours, the people eating their noonday meal (the main meal of the day) and taking their rest. It is precisely the time of day that there would be no interference with the daily obligations. The house-to-house instruction is mentioned only incidentally. (Acts 20:20).

At the end of two years, "all the residents of Asia heard the word of the Lord, both Jews and Greeks" (Acts 19:10). Strong churches were established at Colossae, Hierapolis, and Laodicea in the Lycus Valley almost a hundred miles to the east, and probably at Magnesia, Tralles, and Nyssa along the intervening route; it is almost certain that the other churches of Asia mentioned in Revelation were also founded at this time: Smyrna, Pergamum, Thyatira, Sardis, and Philadelphia; and there are several other places where strong churches were located early in the next century that can probably be traced to the same origin. Since Paul stayed in Ephesus to conduct his program of training, we can only conclude that Paul's disciples were busy in evangelizing the surrounding territory.

Ephesus was an important religious center, the location of the splendid temple of Artemis. This was one of the seven wonders of the ancient world, and attracted pilgrims from far and wide. The religion was a type of nature-worship, honoring Cybele the mother goddess, and far removed from the Greek and Roman idea of the goddess Artemis or Diana who was the symbol of chastity.[19] The religious concept at Ephesus had come from the east, and was spreading into the west, carrying with it grossly immoral sexual practices. The apostle Paul, as a matter of principle had to strike at the roots of this religious system. The way he did it is of considerable interest and importance.

The goddess Artemis was represented as a many-breasted woman, symbol of fertility. Small statues and shrines of the goddess were used in the home and probably carried on the person, perhaps as amulets, much as the more superstitious among us have small figurines of the Madonna on the dashboard of their cars. At Ephesus there was an important industry, involving a number of silversmiths, which thrived on the manufacture of silver shines of Artemis.

One day "there arose no little stir"[20] over the Christian opposition to Artemis. Demetrius, perhaps the leader of the silversmiths' union, agitated his fellow craftsmen with the words, "not only at Ephesus but almost throughout all Asia this Paul has persuaded and turned away a considerable company of people, saying that gods made with hands are not gods. And there is danger not only that this trade of ours may come into disrepute, but also that the temple of the great goddess Artemis may count for nothing, and that she may even be deposed from her magnificence" (Acts 19:26,27). Even allowing for understandable exaggeration such as is common in inflammatory speeches, we must understand that Paul had hurt the business of making Artemis shrines!

The riot got out of hand for a couple of hours, but finally the town clerk restored sufficient quiet to reason with the crowd. What he said should be carefully noted: After pointing out the place of honor that belonged to Ephesus because of the temple of Artemis, he went on to say, "You have brought these men here who are neither sacrilegious nor blasphemers of our goddess" (Acts 19:37).

Think of it! For two years Paul had been preaching in Ephesus. By driving home the principle that "gods made with hands are not gods," he had brought the silversmiths' business to a serious crisis. Yet in public assembly it could be said that he had never blasphemed their goddess!

That is preaching! It avoids name-calling, but gets down to the basic issues. It cuts clean with a sharp edge—but it cuts principles and not persons. Let every preacher and every missionary learn from the apostle Paul!

Notes

1. For a detailed study, see W. M. Ramsay, *The Cities of St. Paul* (London: Hodder and Stoughton, 1907; reprinted, Grand Rapids, Mich.: Baker Book House, 1960), pp. 85-244.

2. The original statement was published in his article, "Tarsus," in Hastings' *Dictionary of the Bible*, vol. 4, p. 687, and corrected in *The Cities of St. Paul* (London: Hodder and Stoughton, 1907), p. 233.

3. Strabo, *Geography*, 14.5.13.

4. Cf. J. Strahan, "Tarsus," Hastings' *Dictionary of the Apostolic Church* (New York: Charles Scribner's Sons, 1915), vol. 2, p. 549.

5. Cf. A. Deissmann, *Light from the Ancient East* (trans. by L. R. M. Strachan; New York: George H. Doran Co., 1927), pp. 238 ff. A careful critical reading is necessary to distinguish this great scholar's a priori judgments from objective scholarship.

6. Cf. J. B. Lightfoot, *Saint Paul's Epistle to the Philippians* (4th ed.; London: Macmillan and Co., 1878), pp. 304 ff.

7. Cf. J. B. Lightfoot, *Biblical Essays* (London: Macmillan and Co., 1893), p. 206. The entire essay, "St. Paul's Preparation for the Ministry," pp. 201-211, is worth reading. For a defense of Paul's classical background, see Evelyn Howell, "St. Paul and the Greek World," *Expository Times* 71 (August 1960), pp. 328-332.

8. Shakespeare has reminded succeeding generations that it was here that Antony and Cleopatra met, the Egyptian beauty's bark navigating the river into the very city. *Antony and Cleopatra*, Act II, Scene ii, lines 192 ff.

9. I have not seen the fact noted that, although Saul might accurately have been classified as a "Hellenist," he refers to himself as a "Hebrew." This implies that his Hebrew characteristics were deliberately emphasized above his Hellenistic characteristics.

10. We have already seen that membership in the Sanhedrin is not definitely implied in Acts 26:10.

11. The debate whether this chapter refers to his preconversion experience or his soul-struggles after conversion can be studied in almost any commentary on Romans. Certain portions seem to me to reflect an earlier struggle, even though the chapter seems to refer to experiences after the conversion.

12. This amazingly rapid spread of rumors and news will astound the Westerner. I have experienced it in the Near East and the Far East, and have been in situations where we were traveling (by horse) thirty miles a day, with no means of communication except word-of-mouth; yet when we arrived at our destinations, word of our coming had preceded us. Our only explanation is that someone was always traveling, bearing the news, while we were halting for food, rest, and other incidents of the route. This is the "grapevine."

13. For a fully detailed, scholarly and thoroughly documented study, see J. G. Machen, *The Origin of Paul's Religion* (London: Hodder and Stoughton, 1921), 329 pp.

14. The site of Derbe as established by Ramsay is now questioned by the discovery of Michael Ballance. Unfortunately, although I covered the region thoroughly, I could find neither Ballance nor anyone who knew where he was exploring. See M. Ballance, "The Site of Derbe: A New Inscription," in *Anatolian Studies* 7 (1957), pp. 147-151.

15. I accept the "south Galatian" theory as fully established, and suggest that travel in Galatia will convince all but the most stubborn. For discussion, see W. M. Ramsay, *A Historical Commentary on St. Paul's Epistle to the Galatians* (New York: G. P. Putnam's Sons, 1900), pp. 103-234; *The Church in the Roman Empire Before* A.D. *170* (London: Hodder and Stoughton, 1893), pp. 16-89; and "Galatia," in Hastings' *Dictionary of the Bible*, vol. 2, pp. 81-89.

16. Cf. Ramsay, *Galatians*, pp. 417-428.

17. The word for "resurrection" in Greek is feminine and perhaps was misunderstood as a female deity (cf. the name Anastasia),

which would explain the curious statement, "He seems to be a preacher of foreign divinities" (Acts 17:18).

18. Whether the address was made before the large council or the smaller one of twelve men, whether it was made in the council chamber or on the hill facing the Acropolis (Mars Hill), I leave for classical scholars to debate. Except for those who demand to see "the exact spot" it makes little difference.

19. It is hardly a mere coincidence that the concept of the "mother of God" (*theotókos*) entered the Christian Church at Ephesus via the Council of A.D. 431. For some stimulating ideas, see W. M. Ramsay, *Pauline and Other Studies* (London: Hodder and Stoughton, 1906), pp. 125-159.

20. The careful reader of Acts will be aware of the fact that Luke often employs litotes, the figure of speech in which an affirmative is expressed by the negative of its contrary. Thus "no little stir" and "no small dissension" actually mean a large commotion and a heated argument.

CHAPTER 7

Barnabas and Mark

We first meet Barnabas in the fourth chapter of
Acts. His name was Joseph, and the apostles had called
him "bar-Nabas," an Aramaic expression meaning "Son
of encouragement (or exhortation)" (Acts 4:36). Barnabas was considered as a prophet and teacher by the
Church (Acts 13:1), and "a good man, full of the Holy
Spirit and of faith" (Acts 11:24).

Barnabas was probably robust and attractive. When
he and Paul were in Lystra, after Paul had healed
a cripple, the people wanted to honor the visitors,
saying, "The gods have come down to us in the likeness
of men!" They thought Barnabas was Zeus and Paul
was Hermes (Acts 14:11-12). Statues of Zeus that have
been preserved from ancient times always present him
as a big, husky, handsome man, the chief of the gods.
Hermes was his messenger.[1]

Barnabas is introduced to us in an account telling
that he sold a field and gave the proceeds to the
apostles, to meet the needs of members of the Early

Church. The Church was attempting to solve a serious problem in a commendable way: Those who had more than they needed sold their goods and gave the money to the apostles; those who had less than they needed received from the apostles to meet their needs (Acts 4:34).[2] Barnabas felt the sense of community, the oneness of the Church, and entered into this demonstration of Christian love.

Barnabas and Saul. After Saul was converted, he went to Jerusalem and attempted to join the disciples (Acts 9:26). Saul had been in Jerusalem before, and the disciples knew all about him: he was the key figure in the persecution that had broken out following the stoning of Stephen (Acts 8:1,3). Saul had become so personally involved in the anti-Christian movement that he had gone to Damascus to persecute the disciples in that city. As a result, the Christians in Jerusalem wanted nothing to do with him. We know, of course, that in the meantime Saul had been converted and had returned to Jerusalem to try to make amends for his former hatred and persecution. They did not know that, or if they had heard it, they did not believe it.

But Barnabas did believe it. He took Saul to the apostles (according to Paul's account, he saw only Peter and James the brother of Jesus; Galatians 1:18,19), and "declared to them how on the road he had seen the Lord, who spoke to him, and how at Damascus he had preached boldly in the name of Jesus" (Acts 9:27). The intercession of Barnabas on Saul's behalf was successful, and Saul was able to initiate a ministry that only had its beginnings in Jerusalem. I think we agree that it was a good thing there was somebody like

Barnabas in the church at Jerusalem. Speaking from the human viewpoint, we would have to admit that if Saul had been unsuccessful in meeting the apostles in Jerusalem (even though, as he asserted, he received nothing to add to his gospel from them), he would have had an extremely difficult if not impossible task. For whether or not he received his gospel from the apostles, he still had to have their credential; his letter to the Galatians, as a matter of fact, depends in a large part for the force of its argument on the fact that his apostleship had been accepted by the apostles (Galatians 2:9).[3]

Again at Antioch, Barnabas demonstrated his faith in Saul of Tarsus.

Barnabas saw the work in Antioch as a demonstration of the grace of God and he rejoiced. He not only rejoiced; he encouraged the work, and as a result, "a large company was added to the Lord" (cf. Acts 11:22-24). More than that, he saw the possibility of expanding the work still further if he could get the right man to help him—and Barnabas knew the right man, and he thought he knew where to find him. So he went to Tarsus to look for Saul (Acts 11:25). It took time, but it resulted in a wonderful year of Christian activity in Antioch, and more than that—but let us not run ahead of the story.

Why did Barnabas think of Saul? We have a ready answer: "Saul was the apostle to the Gentiles." But is that the right answer? Did Barnabas know that at that time? Was Barnabas even thinking in terms of a Gentile ministry at that time? Antioch-on-the-Orontes was a huge city, perhaps one of the most beautiful ever built, and, as third largest city of the

111

empire, capital of the East. There was a large Jewish population there. There were probably many proselytes. Even without thinking of a Gentile ministry, Barnabas saw a great opportunity.[4] But why Saul? What had he been doing?

The letter from the Jerusalem conference was addressed "to the brethren who are of the Gentiles in Antioch and Syria and Cilicia" (Acts 15:23). Syria-and-Cilicia was the name of the Roman province around Antioch, including Tarsus. At the start of his second missionary journey, Paul visited the churches of Syria and Cilicia to strengthen them (Acts 15:41). Where did these churches come from? Paul told the Galatians that after he left Jerusalem he went into "the regions of Syria and Cilicia" (Galatians 1:21). It is my belief that Saul had spent ten years or so preaching in the province around his hometown.[5] I think Barnabas knew something of that work. Barnabas wanted a man with experience for the work that was opening up. Saul was the man.

The church in Antioch was led by the Spirit to commission Barnabas and Saul for the work to which He had called them (Acts 13:2). This was the beginning of organized missionary activity by the Early Church. Their first journey took them to Cyprus and to the south-central portion of Asia Minor.

Why did they go to Cyprus? I think it is obvious: Barnabas came from there. He had friends, and probably relatives, who lived in Cyprus, and he wanted them to hear the gospel. It is a sound missionary principle to start where you have the most in common with your hearers. Before Barnabas and Saul set out on their first missionary journey, they had had at least twelve or thirteen years of Christian service. Even then, they went into an area that one of them knew, and among people with whom they had something in common.

Barnabas and Mark. Barnabas and Saul took with them on their missionary journey a young man named John (Acts 13:5) who was also named Mark (Acts 12:12). The expression, "And they had John to assist [or, minister to] them," is not clear; some think that Mark performed personal services, others think that he helped to catechize the converts.

John Mark was a cousin of Barnabas (Colossians 4:10). Mark's mother Mary (Acts 12:12) was a prominent woman in the church in Jerusalem, and it was in her house that the disciples were praying for Peter when he had been seized by Herod.

We first meet Mark in the year A.D. 44. At that time he was already a Christian and a respected member of the church in Jerusalem. When Barnabas and Saul returned to Antioch, after their famine-visit to Jerusalem (cf. Acts 11:27-30), they took Mark with them (Acts 12:25). As we have seen, they subsequently took Mark on the first missionary journey.

Later, Mark was associated with Peter, and still later, he wrote the Gospel called by his name. According to an early tradition of the Church, Mark served as interpreter on Peter's missionary journeys, and after Peter's death Mark wrote down the words of Peter.[6] This would account for the graphic style of the Gospel of Mark. If the early Christian preachers used catechetical methods of instruction, as seems likely, and if Mark assisted the apostles in this instruction, this would account for formal elements of the second Gospel, which in turn would account for some of the verbal agreements between Mark and other Gospel sources.[7]

When the apostolic mission reached Perga, John Mark turned back. We are not told why, but we know that it caused a serious breach between Paul and Barnabas (Acts 15:39). Various suggestions have been given concerning the cause of Mark's defection. Some think he had experienced a great deal of sickness; it is entirely possible in that part of the world. Some think he was worrying about his mother; that too is possible, and many men have had to give up work they would like to do for the sake of the parents they love. Some think he was afraid; I am inclined to doubt that reason. It seems to me that the "sharp contention" between Paul and Barnabas, however, requires a much more significant reason than any of these expressed. The only reason that would have sufficient magnitude would be one arising from the Judaizer problem. Paul seemed to be able to tolerate almost anything else; but when anyone suggested that anything should be added to the gospel of grace, Paul could find no point of compromise. On this issue he was willing to censure Peter, yes, even Barnabas (Galatians 2:11-14). As I reconstruct the situation, Mark had found Paul's work with Gentiles contrary to his own view of the Law. When it became obvious that they were going to move into territory where Gentiles would predominate, Mark drew the line. He went home.

Barnabas still had faith in Mark. When the Jerusalem conference was over, and Paul said, "Come, let us return and visit the brethren in every city where we proclaimed the word of the Lord" (Acts 15:36), Barnabas said, "Fine; let's take Mark with us." When Paul

114

stubbornly refused, "Barnabas took Mark with him and sailed away to Cyprus, but Paul chose Silas . . ." (Acts 15:39-40). That Mark justified the faith Barnabas put in him, even Paul would admit. Years later, when Paul was in prison waiting for the executioner's sword, he wrote to Timothy, "Get Mark and bring him with you; for he is very useful in serving me" (II Timothy 4:11). What would have happened if Barnabas had not had faith in Mark? Humanly speaking, it is possible that Mark would have dropped out of Christian work altogether. If we had not had his Gospel, we would not have had either Matthew's or Luke's Gospels, for they draw large portions from Mark. But God would not let a man like John Mark get away—that was one of the reasons why He had Barnabas!

Barnabas was not perfect; no one is. The Bible presents its characters without makeup; we see them as they really were—and that is encouragement for the rest of us. Barnabas lost sight of the need of preserving the pure gospel and Christian unity. Under the pressure of Peter and others, he "was carried away by their insincerity," and had to be sternly rebuked by Paul (Galatians 2:13). Paul could not compromise.

Probably it was Barnabas's faith in people that got him into difficulty. Whatever the cause, it did not destroy Paul's respect for him. Paul speaks of Barnabas only in terms of appreciation.

Notes

1. An early tradition of Paul, incidentally, describes him as short, bowlegged, bald-headed, with meeting eyebrows and a long

nose. Cf. The Acts of Paul and Thecla, *The Ante-Nicene Fathers,* vol. 8, p. 487.

2. The Marxist ideal is sometimes quoted, "From each according to his ability, to each according to his need." We have no objection to the ideal; it is the method of enforcing it that is significant: in communism it is the State; in the Church it is love.

3. This side of the argument is often played down in the effort to stress the independency of Paul's gospel. But Paul's whole ministry, his periodic return to Jerusalem and to Antioch to report on his work, and particularly his part in the great discussion at the Jerusalem conference, deny any notion of independency. To him the Church was a body, and no part could say of the other, "I have no need of you" (I Corinthians 12:12-26).

4. The fact that believers were first called "Christians" in Antioch is too well known to need repetition (Acts 11:26). I should point out, however, that the author of Acts is much more careful than I have been in the use of the term, and where I have spoken of "Christians" before this point in the history of the Church, Luke would have used one of several synonyms, "disciples," "believers," "those of the way," etc.

5. R. C. H. Lenski, on the other hand, takes a strongly opposite view in *The Interpretation of the Acts of the Apostles* (Columbus, Ohio: Lutheran Book Concern, 1934), pp. 372-373, 615.

6. For a summary of the numerous sources of this tradition, see H. B. Swete, *The Gospel According to St. Mark* (3d edition; London: Macmillan and Co., 1927), pp. xxiii-xxiv.

7. This is certainly not the place to get into a discussion of Source- and Form-Criticism. For a helpful introduction to the subject, see F. F. Bruce, *The New Testament Documents,* pp. 29-46. On the catechetical motives, see Vincent Taylor, *The Gospel According to St. Mark* (London: Macmillan and Co., 1952), p. 133.

CHAPTER 8

Luke

There is only one Gentile author included in the Bible: Luke, who wrote the third Gospel and Acts. That Luke was a Gentile is clearly indicated in Colossians, where Aristarchus, Mark, and Jesus Justus are distinguished from Epaphras, Luke, and Demas, the first three being "the only men of the circumcision among my fellow workers" (Colossians 4:11), and therefore the only Jews.[1] The writings of this lone Gentile, which comprise the largest part of the New Testament by any single writer, are magnificent literature. Even a man who is not interested in the spiritual values of the writings will appreciate the literary qualities, the composition, style, and other elements, of Luke's works. Luke's appreciation of beauty is evident often, but especially in the fact that he alone of the New Testament writers recorded the hymns, *Benedic-*

tus, Magnificat, and *Nunc Dimittis,* hymns which have become part of the liturgy of the Church.

Luke was a scientific man and a doctor. Science is the process of observation, comparison, control, and deduction, or the abstracting of principles. That method was already well known in the Greek world and particularly in the medical world, and Luke was heir to a science of medicine that could compare favorably with any medical practice up to the early part of the last century. The body had been dissected, and the brain, nervous system and circulatory system had been explored (although some of the theories make us smile today). The center of medical science was along the Ionian coast of the Aegean Sea—which is where Luke seems to have spent much of his life.

According to some scholars, Luke was born in Syrian Antioch. He certainly shows great familiarity with Antioch and with the church there. Others think that Luke came from Philippi in Macedonia. We first cross his trail in Troas and he is personally involved in the apostolic mission to Philippi. Luke was apparently a Christian before he met Paul, but we have no knowledge of his conversion. There is some rather convincing evidence that Luke was familiar with the sea and with ships; and the suggestion that he was at one time a ship's doctor would fit in with this evidence. We know that Paul had some kind of affliction that he refers to, and the suggestion has been made that Luke was called in to treat Paul. All these suggestions are attractive—but we must bear in mind that they are only suggestions, not established facts.

Luke shows great interest in healing. Of the four Gospel writers, he is the only one to tell of the good

120

Samaritan (Luke 10:25-37), the casting out of the demons (Luke 11:14-36), the healing of the man with dropsy (Luke 14:1-6), the healing of the woman with the unclean spirit (Luke 13:10-17), and the cleansing of the ten lepers (Luke 17:11-19). Likewise in Acts, he tells of the healing of the lame man at the Temple gate (Acts 3:1-8), the healing of Aeneas (Acts 9:33,34), the healing of the cripple at Lystra (Acts 14:8-10), the resuscitation of Eutychus at Troas (Acts 20:9-12), and the curing of Publius' father on Malta (Acts 28:7-10).

Luke shows a deep interest in women and children, which would also be true of a medical doctor. Of the Gospel writers, Luke alone records the details of the birth stories and the childhood details (Luke 1:5—2:52). He alone tells of the raising of the widow's son (Luke 7:11-17), of the anointing of Jesus by the sinful woman (Luke 7:36-50); he alone tells the story of Martha and Mary (Luke 10:38-42), and the parable of the importunate widow (Luke 18:1-14). Likewise in Acts, women are included at numerous points in the story of the Early Church.

In the account of Paul's healing ministry on Malta there is an indication that Luke may have added his medical skill to Paul's miraculous healing. Two different Greek words are used: the first in the statement "and Paul visited him and prayed, and putting his hands on him healed him" (Acts 28:8), where the word conveys the idea of healing brought to its completion; the second word is used in the next verse, "the rest of the people on the island who had diseases also came and were cured" (Acts 28:9), where the word conveys the idea of the healing process from its beginning.[2]

We might paraphrase by saying that Paul healed the first, Paul and Luke treated and cured the others. Is this why Luke records, "They presented many gifts to us"?

Luke the historian. In the providence of God this man with scientifically trained powers of observation became the historian of the Early Church. The opening of his Gospel gives an idea of his method and purpose: "Inasmuch as many have undertaken to compile a narrative of the things which have been accomplished among us, just as they were delivered to us by those who from the beginning were eyewitnesses and ministers of the word, it seemed good to me also, having followed all things closely for some time past, to write an orderly account for you . . ." (Luke 1:1-3).

Luke states at once in the Gospel that he was not an eyewitness; he used available sources. There are some believers who hold such a narrow view of inspiration that they feel we dishonor the Holy Spirit when we speak of sources. The historic view of inspiration teaches that the Holy Spirit inspired men in their use of materials, including sources.

In the case of Acts, on the other hand, Luke was an eyewitness of some of the things he had recorded. In Acts 16:10, the first person pronoun "we" slips unobtrusively into the record, and continues to verse 17; the account then is told in the third person ("he" or "they"). In Acts 20:5 another "we" section occurs, continuing to Acts 21:25; and a third "we" section is found from Acts 27:2 to 28:16. Now the name of Luke does not occur in the book of Acts. The question therefore naturally arises: How do we know that "we" is intended to include Luke; is there any way to check on this? There is. The periods covered by the "we" passages are the following: from Troas to Philippi on the second missionary journey, from Philippi to Caesarea on the third journey, and from Caesarea to Rome on the first journey to Rome. We can find in the writings of Paul indications of these periods and references to his associates. Luke is mentioned in the New Testament only three times: two of these references are from the Roman imprisonment (Colossians 4:14; Philemon 23), which agrees with the third "we" section.

For the balance of the material in Acts, Luke used sources. From the itinerary sketched by the "we" sections, we can tell with reasonable certainty what some of these sources may have been. There was Paul, of course, who could have told Luke all about the stoning of Stephen, his own conversion, the first missionary journey, the Jerusalem conference, and all the other details that involved Paul when Luke was not present personally. There was Silas, who certainly knew important details of the Jerusalem church, for he was one of the leaders there (Acts 15:22). At Caesarea there was Philip the evangelist (Acts 21:8), who surely knew the details of the choosing of the Seven (the deacons) and the conversion of the Ethiopian, as well as the story of Simon Magus and other incidents in Samaria (Acts 6 and 8). Since Luke was present in Caesarea both at the end of the third journey and at the beginning of the journey to Rome, it is a reasonable supposition that he remained in the general area for the intervening two years, and it is also reasonable to suppose that he used some of this time to collect material for the third Gospel. The sources for this material would be able to furnish information for the remainder of the early chapters of Acts.

Luke has gathered together in Acts an amazing mass of detail. According to one scholar, one hundred and ten persons are named in Acts.[3] Place names, geographical details, official names and titles, with other factual data, are found on every page. In 1880, William M. Ramsay made his first visit to Asia Minor, the beginning of research that was to occupy him for the next thirty-four years. He was a classics scholar, with a critical view of the Scriptures. As he became acquainted with detail after detail, fact after fact, he came to realize that Luke was the master historian. In 1911 Ramsay stated: "Every person is found just where he ought to be: proconsuls in senatorial provinces, asiarchs in Ephesus, strategoi in Philippi, politarchs in Thessalonica, magicians and soothsayers everywhere."[4]

Luke has preserved the color, the character, the verisimilitude of widely different persons and situations. The speeches he has preserved retain the personal characteristics of the speakers. The local customs are accurately reflected. Life is filled with endless variety; Luke has observed that variety, and recorded the details with unerring eye and ear. Peter is Peter and Paul is Paul; Antioch is Antioch and Athens is Athens. Try to record the details of your travels sometime (I have tried, often!), and you will appreciate Luke as never before. Try to portray an imaginary journey, and you will realize how empty is the argument that Luke wrote fiction. Hollywood hired technical advisors for the production of a biblical film and when they were finished, scholars in the audience laughed at the errors in detail. Luke had no staff of technical advisors, no research library, no electronic equipment. And Sir William Ramsay, who had few peers in classical studies and none in the historical geography of Asia Minor, could find no flaw in Luke's production! Luke was a scientifically trained historian.

Luke the evangelist. Luke wrote his books not just to write, but to save a soul. Scholars are generally convinced that he had in mind a larger circle of readers—and possibly he did. But the undeniable fact is that he addressed both works to Theophilus for the express purpose of setting the truth before Theophilus. He wanted to present the story of Jesus Christ in the most convincing form, which was to tell the truth with beauty and clarity; likewise he wanted to present the story of the origin of the Christian faith. Luke was at heart an evangelist. He wanted to proclaim the Evangel, the Good News.

Luke's interest in the gospel of salvation, however, is not speculation. It is firmly established. His Gospel alone records the parables of the lost coin, the lost sheep, and the prodigal son and his lost brother (Luke 15). His Gospel alone tells the story of Zacchaeus, who climbed a tree to see Jesus, and whose house Jesus graced with the words: "Today salvation has come to this house. . . . For the Son of man came to seek and to save the lost" (see Luke 19:1-10). The book of Acts is the message of salvation from beginning to end. The disciples waited until they had received the Holy Spirit; then they began the preaching of the gospel. Stephen was chosen to serve tables, but he preached the gospel. Saul was the persecutor of the Church, but when the risen Lord appeared to him he began at once to preach the gospel. To see this truth is to know Luke the evangelist.

Doctor Luke should be an inspiration and a challenge to any medical doctor; in fact, to any man of a scientific mind, for he combines the rare gifts of scientific training and evangelical passion, the care of the body and the care of the soul.

Notes

1. In spite of the clear statement in Scripture, an occasional author, trying to defend the theory that Romans 3:2 requires that all Scripture writers be Jews, insists that Luke was a Jew. Romans 3:2 refers to the Old Testament. Moreover, if God was breaking down the wall that separated Jews and Gentiles, why would this not also apply to the writers of Scripture?

2. The first word is from *iáomai* "to heal," the second from *therapeúō* "to treat medically, to cure."

3. Lenski, *Interpretation of the Acts of the Apostles*, p. 5.

4. W. M. Ramsay, *The Bearing of Recent Discovery on the Trustworthiness of the New Testament* (2d edition; London: Hodder and Stoughton, 1915; reprinted Grand Rapids, Mich.: Baker Book House, 1953), pp. 96-97. The lecture was delivered in 1911.

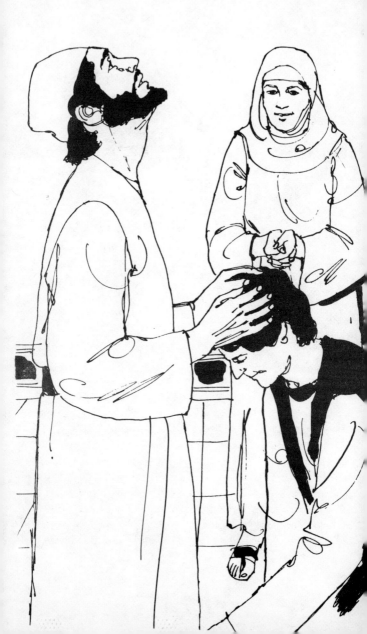

CHAPTER 9

Timothy and Titus

Luke gives us a brief description of Timothy when he first appears in Acts: "And he [Paul] came also to Derbe and to Lystra. A disciple was there, named Timothy, the son of a Jewish woman who was a believer; but his father was a Greek. He was well spoken of by the brethren at Lystra and Iconium" (Acts 16:1,2). The way the statement is worded, Timothy may have been living at either Lystra or Derbe.[1] The time was early in the second missionary journey, perhaps A.D. 50. Luke's sentence structure—an important point when reading an author who is so careful in such matters—suggests not only that Timothy's father was a Greek, whereas his mother was a Jewess, but also that Timothy's father was not a believer. Since Timothy had not been circumcised (cf. Acts 16:3), we may suppose that the father was not sympathetic to the mother's religious views and perhaps had even forbidden the religious rite.

It is generally assumed that Timothy was converted to Christianity by Paul. This is based on the way Paul refers to his young colleague; for example, "my true child in the faith" (I Timothy 1:2), and "my beloved and faithful child in the Lord" (I Corinthians 4:17). Once again, however, I would suggest that we do not accept as an established fact what is only a very good suggestion. In II Timothy 3:15 there is a suggestion that Timothy may have received his faith from his mother. Paul's references to Timothy as his "child in the faith" would be sufficiently explained, I believe, by the fact that Paul trained Timothy in Christian doctrine and practice.

How old Timothy was at the time we are not told. Nearly twenty years later Paul addressed Timothy as a young man—but what is a "young man"? To a twenty-year-old, a man of forty is not young; to a man of sixty or seventy, the forty-year-old man is still young. We suppose that Timothy was in his teens when Paul first visited Lystra and Derbe; that he was perhaps in his early twenties at the time of Paul's second visit—which would make him forty or forty-five when the Pastoral Epistles were written.

When Paul returned to Timothy's hometown on his second missionary journey, he was impressed with the reports of Timothy's Christian faith and life, and desired to take Timothy along with him. On the first journey, we remember, Paul and Barnabas had started out with young John Mark as their helper. Timothy would stand in the same relationship to the team of Paul and Silas. Timothy's mother agreed, obviously, and the Church ordained the young man by the laying on of hands (compare II Timothy 1:6 with I Timothy 4:14).

We can trace Timothy's itinerary with some detail. He went to Europe with Paul, Silas, and Luke, but was apparently not jailed with Paul and Silas in Philippi (Acts 16:19). Luke seems to have stayed in Philippi when the other three moved west along the Egnatian Road to Thessalonica. When Paul and Silas were sent off to neighboring Beroea by night, Timothy seems to have remained in Thessalonica, but later joined the apostles in Beroea (cf. Acts 17:10,14); Timothy and Silas stayed there when Paul moved on to Athens. Later Paul sent Timothy to Thessalonica (it would seem that Timothy had meanwhile rejoined Paul at Athens, but this is not clear), in order to get news about his recent converts and to establish them in the faith (I Thessalonians 3:1-2). After that, Timothy and Silas joined Paul in Corinth (Acts 18:5), and Paul sent the first of his letters to the Thessalonians (I Thessalonians 3:6), rejoicing over the news which Timothy had brought. It is possible that Timothy acted both as Paul's amanuensis and emissary, writing the letter for Paul and delivering it; then returning with a reply that occasioned the second letter to Thessalonica.

The next time we hear of Timothy he was in Ephesus with Paul, and Paul was sending him and Erastus to Macedonia, where Thessalonica is located (Acts 19:22). Still later, Paul sent Timothy from Ephesus to Corinth to handle some of the difficult matters in that church (I Corinthians 4:17). The last time Timothy is mentioned in Acts is at Troas with the group that was planning to carry an offering from the Gentile churches to the needy Jewish Christians at Jerusalem (Acts 20:4).

According to the salutations of the Prison Epistles, Timothy was with Paul during the first Roman imprisonment (cf. Colossians 1:1; Philippians 1:1; Philemon 1). Then, if we are correct in following the tradition that Paul was released from prison, Timothy went to Ephesus with Paul and was left there to carry on the work in that city (I Timothy 1:3). He was imprisoned, where and when we do not know, and subsequently released (Hebrews 13:23), and later, according to tradition, martyred at Ephesus under Domitian after having served as the first bishop of Ephesus.[2]

Timothy was doubtless the closest of Paul's associates, with perhaps the exception of Luke. He is mentioned in the opening salutation of six of Paul's epistles as coauthor, and two others are addressed to him.

Timothy and Titus. Titus is one of the outstanding men in the New Testament Church. He was of Gentile parents (Galatians 2:3), and was taken to Jerusalem by Paul at the time of the Judaizer controversy (Galatians 2:1). Titus was "Exhibit A"—evidence that could be examined; living proof that a Gentile who had not come under the Law of Moses could still demonstrate the fruits of the Spirit that were the sign of a regenerate man in Christ.

Titus comes into our story about Timothy in connection with the problems in the Corinthian Church. Timothy, we learned, had been sent to Corinth by

Paul to take care of grave difficulties in that church, difficulties of moral, doctrinal, and administrative nature. To read the letters to the Corinthians is to discover how complex the problems were. And Timothy failed in the mission. He failed not because of any lack of ability, but because of lack of experience: he was just too young. The church in Corinth despised his youth, and were hostile because Paul himself had not visited them (see I Corinthians 4:17-18 and compare I Corinthians 16:10-11). Perhaps that was why Paul on a later occasion said to Timothy, "Let no one despise your youth" (I Timothy 4:12).

If we take the trouble to check the chronological details, we shall find that this was about A.D. 55. Timothy had been in Paul's company almost constantly for about five years. He had traveled widely, had undergone all sorts of experiences with Paul and with Silas; he had even been sent on missions alone by Paul, such as those to Thessalonica. He was by this time probably twenty-five years old, and a veteran of five years' service. In our modern day, we take young fellows and girls who have had little or no training in Christian service and send them into some of the most difficult situations in the world—then we wonder why they sometimes fail. They fail because we are expecting young people to do the work of mature and experienced workers. With far more preparation and experience, Timothy failed. But failure under such circumstances is no disgrace.

Titus, however, succeeded. Paul was comforted by the news that Titus brought and by the fact that he had been so well received in the Corinthian Church (cf. II Corinthians 7:5-7). Titus was probably somewhat older than Timothy (compare Titus 2:15 with I Timothy 4:12), and he had had a few more years' experience. Possibly he had certain personal qualifications that Timothy lacked, as, for example, self-confidence or boldness. It is even possible that Timothy had, knowingly or unknowingly, prepared the way for Titus; the Corinthians had had time to regret how they had treated Timothy and may have determined to act toward Titus in a more Christian manner. Whatever the reasons, we know that an affection developed between Titus and the Corinthian Church that brought joy to Paul's heart (cf. II Corinthians 7:13-14; 8:16).

After Paul was released from the Roman imprisonment, he took Titus and Timothy on some part of his further travels. He left Timothy in Ephesus, as we have seen; and he left Titus in Crete (Titus 1:5). That in itself is to me an amazing testimony of Paul's confidence in these two men. Ephesus was, by Paul's own estimate, one of the most strategically important cities of the Empire. It was not without its difficulties, particularly with reference to the hostility of those who were devoted to the goddess Artemis. Later, as we find from Second Timothy and corroborated by Revelation 2:2-6, strong reaction set in against the gospel. Yet Paul was willing to entrust the situation to Timothy. Likewise Crete was one of the more difficult regions in the Empire, as we know from references in the literature of the day. Paul was willing to place the work there in the care of Titus.

Timothy and the Church. We are beginning to get, through the experiences of Timothy, a different view of the Church. Up until this point, we have been seeing the Church of the first generation. It was the Church of the apostles, the Church of those who had known Jesus according to the flesh, or had (in the case of Paul) been granted a personal experience of the risen Christ. But with Timothy, and doubtless also with Titus, we are moving into the next generation: this is "second generation Christianity," with all its new problems. The Church that we see in the experiences of Timothy is the Church in its ongoing history, after the apostles have begun to depart from the scene.

Of course the apostles were not yet gone; but Paul was anxiously making preparations for the day when he would be. He was setting up Timothy and Titus (and were there others, of whom these are typical?) in strategic locations because he knew that the hour of his departure was at hand. He was writing letters to them (and shall we not assume that he expected others to read these letters?) in order to strengthen them for the work of the next generation.

Timothy was not an apostle; that is made clear in Colossians 1:1. He was never looked upon as a successor to Paul, and he was never portrayed as having the authority of an apostle. Read the letters to Timothy and Titus, and notice that such authority remained in the apostolic office and was not conferred on younger ministers. Yet there is authority (cf. I Timothy 4:11, 14): it is the authority of the gospel.

Through Timothy we learn something about the nature of the Church. It is God's family (I Timothy 3:5, 15). Its members are called "brothers" (I Timothy 4:6), "believers" (I Timothy 4:12; 5:16), and "holy ones" (or "saints," I Timothy 5:10). These words define their relationship to one another: they are brothers;

their relationship to God: they are believers; and their relationship to the world: they are holy, set apart from sin for lives of purity.

Our first responsibility, as was Timothy's, is to guard the faith that is in us. "You then, my son, be strong in the grace that is in Christ Jesus" (II Timothy 2:1). If you are concerned by apostasy in the world, look to your own spiritual life. Make sure that it is strong.

The second responsibility that Paul laid upon Timothy was to train up faithful successors. "What you have heard from me before many witnesses entrust to faithful men who will be able to teach others also" (II Timothy 2:2).

The third responsibility was to trust God. "God's firm foundation stands, bearing this seal: 'The Lord knows those who are his,' and, 'Let every one who names the name of the Lord depart from iniquity'" (II Timothy 2:19).

The fourth responsibility, and by no means the least important, was to stay out of arguments. "Have nothing to do with stupid, senseless controversies; you know that they breed quarrels. And the Lord's servant must not be quarrelsome but kindly to every one, an apt teacher, forbearing, correcting his opponents with gentleness. God may perhaps grant that they will repent and come to know the truth" (II Timothy 2:23-25). Righteousness, faith, love, and peace will have far greater effect upon the opponents than argument (cf. II Timothy 2:22).

All these responsibilities can be summarized in one charge: "Preach the word, be urgent in season and out of season, convince, rebuke, and exhort, be unfailing in patience and in teaching" (II Timothy 4:2).

Notes

1. F. F. Bruce, for example, chooses Lystra on the basis of its occurrence in both sentences (*The Book of the Acts,* p. 321). It would be equally logical to assume that Derbe was Timothy's home, since his reputation at Lystra and Iconium is mentioned. See also Acts 20:4. The point is hardly worth debating.

2. Eusebius, *Ecclesiastical History* 3.4; Nicephorus, *Ecclesiastical History* 3.11. The latter reference is from *The Fathers of the Church,* edited by R. J. Defarrari, vol. 19, *Eusebius Pamphili, Ecclesiastical History* (New York: Fathers of the Church, Inc., 1953), p. 142, n. 6; I have been unable to verify the reference.

CHAPTER 10

Thomas

We usually speak of Thomas as a doubter: "doubting Thomas." I would like to present him as the believer. The words of his faith constitute the fullest statement of faith expressed in the gospels: "My Lord and my God" (John 20:28).

Thomas and Jesus. Thomas was a doubter; I would not deny that. But even his doubts must be set against the background of his faith. Thomas was one of the Twelve, but before he became one of the Twelve, he had to be one of the disciples. Let the implications sink in, and you will realize that somewhere along the way, and it must have been early in Jesus' ministry, Thomas had heard the call of Jesus and had cast his lot in with Him. Jesus had observed him carefully, as He had observed the others, and after a night in prayer had chosen Thomas as one of that group to whom would be given the tremendous and awful responsibility of evangelizing the world. This should convince us of the worth of this man.

There are three short references to Thomas, all of them in John. The first is in the eleventh chapter, in connection with the illness of Lazarus and the events pertaining to it. Jesus and His apostles were beyond the Jordan, safely beyond the reach of those who were seeking to destroy Him; for, as we know, Jesus had a sense of timing whereby His death must occur on the day of the great sacrifice, the Passover. Word had been sent to Jesus that Lazarus was ill, and Jesus had delayed going to Bethany. Then He announced to the disciples that "Lazarus is dead. . . . let us go to him" (John 11:14,15). At this point, Thomas comes into the picture, saying, "Let us also go, that we may die with him" (John 11:16).

It is clear that Thomas did not understand Jesus, and I am not sure I understand Thomas. Thomas may have thought that by the expression, "Let us go to him," Jesus was implying that they should join Lazarus in death. Such an idea he would have gotten, I think, from Jesus' teachings about the suffering and death that must occur at Jerusalem. Or it may be that Thomas was simply referring to the danger that a trip to the vicinity of Jerusalem would incur: it would be sealing their own death warrants. But regardless of what Thomas implied, there can be no doubt that Thomas was declaring his loyalty to the Master, and his willingness to die, if necessary, for the Master.

The second reference to Thomas is found in the fourteenth chapter of John. This was only a short time after the resurrection of Lazarus, and the dinner given in honor of Jesus had brought a crowd of people to see Lazarus also (cf. John 12:9). The following day had been exciting, with the triumphal entry of Jesus into Jerusalem; that had been followed by two days of activity in Jerusalem, as Jesus sought desperately to bring the city to its senses, while the religious leaders sought to trap Him into some statement or action that could be used as a capital charge against Him. The sands of time were running out rapidly, and Jesus had gathered His own in the Upper Room for the parting words of instruction.

"Let not your hearts be troubled," He said; "believe in God, believe also in me. In my Father's house are many rooms; if it were not so, would I have told you that I go to prepare a place for you? And when I go and prepare a place for you, I will come again and will take you to myself, that where I am you may be also. And you know the way where I am going" (John 14:1-4). Thomas interrupted: "Lord, we do not know where you are going; how can we know the way?"

Thomas may have understood that Jesus was referring to His death, and may have been seeking more light on the "where" and the "way." If Jesus had intended to follow up this line of inquiry, He was interrupted by Philip's question (John 14:8 ff.). Most of us, I am sure, wish that Jesus had said more about His Father's house—but He told us all He wants us to know, and all we need to know.

The third reference to Thomas is in the twentieth chapter of John. The resurrection of Jesus had taken place. It was the evening of resurrection day, the first

Easter Sunday, and there was much excitement among the Eleven—Judas had removed himself not only from the apostolic band but from this life as well—for there were strange reports that Jesus was alive. He had been seen by Peter. Two disciples from Emmaus reported walking and talking with Jesus. The women's stories about the empty tomb and the angelic messages were being recounted. And as a result, the apostles, who had been scattered by the terrible tragedy of the cross, had gathered together, still fearsome of the spirit of hostility in the city. Suddenly, Jesus was in their midst. His first words were, "Peace be with you." Then He showed them the tokens of His passion, His hands and side.[1] Thomas was not present.

When the disciples found Thomas, they told him, "We have seen the Lord." Thomas said, "Unless I see in his hands the print of the nails, and place my finger in the mark of the nails, and place my hand in his side, I will not believe" (John 20:25).

Thomas and his doubts. Have you ever thought about the different kinds of doubt? There is one word,[2] sometimes translated "doubt," that means "perplexity, inability to comprehend." Like the Latin word *dubitare*, from which we get our word "doubt," it has a basic meaning related to "way," except that the Latin literally means "to go two ways," whereas the Greek means, "without a way." This is the word used of the women at the empty tomb: they were "perplexed" (Luke 24:4); this is the word used of the disciples when Jesus announced, "One of you will betray me" (John 13:21); a similar but stronger word is used of Herod, when he heard reports that John the Baptist was alive again

142

(Luke 9:7), and again of the crowd in Jerusalem when they heard the apostles speaking with tongues (Acts 2:12). In all cases, they were stopped, they did not know which way to turn for a solution to the situation confronting them.

A second word for "doubt" has more the meaning of "weakening or loss of faith."[3] Faith was already present, but then began to fail. The word is used of Peter, after he had started to walk on the water, and then asked himself, "What am I doing here?" Jesus said to him, "Why did you doubt?" (Matthew 14:31). The word is also used of the disciples, when they met with the risen Lord: "And when they saw him they worshiped him; but some doubted" (Matthew 28:17).

The third word originally meant "to discriminate, decide," and in Hellenistic Greek came to mean "to be divided in mind, hesitate, doubt."[4] It is used when God instructed Peter concerning the men sent by Cornelius: "accompany them without hesitation"—I suppose we might translate it, "without allowing your critical judgment to hold you back by doubting My word" (Acts 10:20).

None of these words is used about Thomas, and none of them truly fits the situation.

If we turn to the idea of "unbelief," we find again that there are several kinds of unbelief, although in this case we do not find the distinction in the use of different Greek words. Rather, the differentiation must be sought in how the word is used.[5] There is a kind of unbelief that might be termed scientific skepticism. It says, "I do not believe, because there is insufficient evidence to convince me." It is a judgment that may be challenged by others who are convinced that there

143

is sufficient evidence, but we must recognize the fact that the scientist has been trained to verify his observations, and the once-for-all (the miracle, the unique Son, the single resurrection, etc.) is not repeatable and therefore not verifiable by the scientist. The historian, on the other hand, must accept hearsay evidence; his verification is only an effort to check the accuracy of the witnesses. This skeptical unbelief is perhaps illustrated by the disciples, when the women reported their experiences at the garden tomb to the apostles: "but these words seemed to them an idle tale, and they did not believe [literally, they disbelieved] them" (Luke 24:11).

A second kind of unbelief is deliberate rejection. Paul uses the noun form of the word, "unbelievers," quite often in his Corinthian letters, to designate non-Christians (see I Corinthians 7:12-15; II Corinthians 6:14,15, etc.), but the deliberateness of the rejection is more sharply etched in a statement such as that reported at the close of Acts: "And some were convinced by what he said, while others disbelieved" (Acts 28:24). Paul's use of a quotation from Isaiah (6:9-10) serves to define further the kind of disbelief that is intended.

A third kind of unbelief is perhaps best illustrated by the father of the demon-possessed boy. Jesus said to him, "All things are possible to him who believes," and the father replied, "I believe; help my unbelief!" (Mark 9:23,24). It is almost like saying, "I have faith; but I haven't yet come to the place where I have real faith." There is nothing essentially wrong with this kind of unbelief, provided we do not become established in it. But if we become content with unbelief, we shall one day find ourselves confronted with the horrible judgment prepared for the cowardly, the faithless, murderers, liars, and others like them (see Revelation 21:8).

What was Thomas' characteristic? It was not doubt. It could hardly be called skepticism. In the light of what happened when he was confronted with the evidence, we cannot call it deliberate disbelief. The best term is simply unbelief. Jesus confronted Thomas, and said, "Put your finger here, and see my hands; and put out your hand, and place it in my side; do not be faithless, but believing" (John 20:27).[6]

Thomas and his faith. The resurrection of Jesus Christ is central in the faith of the Christian Church. Carefully defined and clearly understood, it would be possible to say that without the resurrection of Jesus Christ there is no Christian faith. This is what the apostle Paul says in his great chapter on the resurrection. Read it carefully: "If Christ has not been raised, then our preaching is in vain and your faith is in vain. . . . If Christ has not been raised, your faith is futile and you are still in your sins" (I Corinthians 15:14, 17).

This has always been the unwavering and unquestioned faith of the Church. There has never been a doctrinal controversy on the subject of the resurrection of Christ.[7] The Church discussed the natures of Christ, the Trinity, the procession of the Holy Spirit, and many other subjects, but it was unanimous in the declaration that on the third day Christ rose again. The person who denies the resurrection of Christ places himself outside the faith of the historic Christian Church just as surely as does the man who denies the incarnation.

In the hazy thinking and careless usage of words that characterize too much of modern religious thought and writing, immortality is often confused with resurrection. Immortality is a state of being not mortal, not subject to death. Resurrection is an act, a change, a rising from the dead to newness of life. What could the statement "on the third day He was immortal" possibly mean? If He was immortal on the third day, He was equally immortal on the second and the fourth. Moreover, what is the significance of the resurrection appearances of Jesus to His apostles? And that brings us back to Thomas. Thomas was not convinced by the accounts that he heard. He wanted evidence before he was willing to commit himself in faith. What kind of evidence was available?

First, either Jesus died on the cross, or He did not die. If He did not die, then what happened to Him? The "swoon" theory supplies the answer: He revived in the cool of the tomb. Pushing aside the stone,[8] He made His way to the apostles, who nursed Him back to health. Apart from the hypocrisy involved in apostles who would report His resurrection knowing the truth, how does this fit with the experience of Thomas?

Second, if Jesus died on the cross, either His body was found in the tomb, or the tomb was found empty. His body was not found in the tomb: that is the testimony of the women and also of Peter and John (see Mark 16:5; John 20:6); further, it is corroborated by the fact that His enemies did not produce the body.

Third, if an empty tomb was found, it was either the wrong tomb or the right one. The right one was identified by a seal and a guard of soldiers (Matthew

146

27:66). Independent groups or individuals found their way to a common point: Mary Magdalene, very early in the morning, then Peter and John, and still later the women mentioned in Mark (see John 20:1 ff.; Mark 16:1 ff.)—and their testimony concurs. They could not all have made the same mistake. Moreover, the testimony of the soldiers substantiates this point (Matthew 28:11).

Fourth, if the tomb was found empty, the body either was taken or rose. If it was taken, it was taken either by enemies or friends; if by enemies, they would have produced it and silenced the apostolic preaching of the resurrection; if by friends, then we have, as many have recognized, the psychological impossibility of apostles suffering martyrdom for what they knew was not true. The story that the disciples had stolen the body was tried at the very outset (see Matthew 28:11-15), and convinced no one. Except for some cheap pulp writings or some anti-Christian movements, this theory has been given up. And again, we must ask, what about Thomas? Can we suppose that he who refused to be convinced by apostolic testimony could be convinced by apostolic fraud?

That brings us to the last step of the logical process: Jesus Christ rose from the dead. Either He was seen thereafter, or He was not seen. Peter says he saw Him; the two from Emmaus claim they saw Him; the women saw Him; the rest of the apostles saw Him. Paul, having started out as a bitter opponent of the movement, declared that Jesus appeared "to more than five hundred brethren at one time," most of whom were still alive when he wrote those words (I Corinthians 15:6). But what about Thomas? Thomas refused to believe the testimony of anyone else—even that of his closest friends. Then came the night when Jesus appeared to him, challenged him to put his unbelief to the test by touching the wounds still visible, and Thomas yielded: "My Lord and my God!"

Thomas and his followers. Thomas faced the problem of faith for all honest unbelievers. Jesus knew that there would be others like Thomas: "Have you believed because you have seen me? Blessed are those who have not seen and yet believe" (John 20:29).

Some doubters do not deserve to be classed with Thomas: those who are superficial and are not interested in the evidence; sophomoric persons who are proud of being skeptics and do not want to see any evidence that will force them to change their minds; and the disbelievers, who flatly reject all evidence.

But there are others who can be called honest doubters. They do not believe the evidence is sufficient, or they have not considered the evidence. They are willing to consider it, and Thomas would be the first to invite them to sit down while he tells them his experience.

Notes

1. Traditionally, there were five wounds: the hands, the side, and the feet. Strangely enough, Scripture nowhere mentions any nailing of the feet of Jesus!

2. In Greek, *aporô.* Quite similar in meaning is *diaporô.*

3. The Greek word is *distázō*, which is somewhat like the Latin *dubitare* in its formation from the word for "two."

4. In Greek, *diakri nō.*

5. In Greek, the word is *ápistos* ("without faith") and its derivatives.

6. The play on words in Greek (*ápistos* and *pistós*) would be better brought out if translated, "do not be believing-less, but believing" or "do not be without faith, but with faith."

7. An examination of R. Seeberg's two-volume *Text-Book of the History of Doctrines* (Philadelphia: Lutheran Publication Society, 1904), for example, will show that the word "resurrection" is not even in the index. The only discussions of the subject of resurrection that took place concerned the nature of our bodies in the final resurrection. I do not consider modern unbelief to be in the category of a doctrinal controversy.

8. The theory was first proposed in ignorance of the nature of such stones. They roll in deep-cut grooves, and fall into a socket when closed. It would take two healthy men to move such a stone, as the women knew (Mark 16:3).

CHAPTER 11

John

Theologians today are not high on the list of the
world's most popular figures. Let a preacher announce
that he is planning to give a series of theological
lectures, and the people stay away in droves. Scientists,
on the other hand, are quite popular. Yet the strange
and simple fact is that theologians are, or ought to
be, scientists. That statement needs explaining, I know.
A scientist is one who has learned to apply scientific
method, which is to observe, record, compare, control,
and draw whatever conclusions are valid. The theologian ("theology," as the word implies, is the orderly
study of God) should observe, record, compare, control,
and draw conclusions concerning what he can learn
about God.[1]

151

The Bible, we are told, does not contain theology. In a sense, this is true. Neither does the world contain geology or chemistry. But the world does contain the data which the scientist can arrange into the science of geology or chemistry; and the Bible and the world likewise contain the data which the theologian can arrange in orderly and systematic manner—which is theology. Theology, by its very nature, is fraught with the dangers of subjectivism. The theologian, if he is not extremely careful, will record his impressions or opinions about God and the spiritual world, and think that these are objective data; and the scientist, of course, becomes impatient with him.

The theologian, therefore, should have a long life, for he has many observations to make; he should be intimately acquainted with God, not only in mystical immediacy, but also in some way that is sensuously verifiable; and he should be gifted in ability to make known his conclusions in such a way that others will understand him.

John had these qualifications.[2] He lived to about one hundred years of age. He was a mystic, and yet he knew the Incarnate Son of God in the flesh (cf. I John 1:1). His Gospel is, beyond any argument, a beautiful book, a book that presents theological concepts in the simplest form, a book that men have read and loved and understood—at least sufficiently to give them satisfaction of soul.

John and the Holy Spirit. The most extensive, and in fact the only satisfactory teachings on the Holy Spirit in the Gospels are in the Gospel of John. On the last night before His death, Jesus said, "These things I have spoken to you, while I am still with you. But the Counselor, the Holy Spirit, whom the Father will send in my name, he will teach you all things, and bring to your remembrance all that I have said to you" (John 14:25,26). Perhaps John did not particularly notice those words when they were spoken—no one else recorded them—but sixty-five years or so later, he remembered them as clearly as if they had just been uttered. Why? To reply that this is how the mind works, that as we grow older we tend to remember details of our earlier life, is only part of the answer. John remembered because the Holy Spirit helped him to remember. That is what the Holy Spirit is for.

This certainly does not mean that the Holy Spirit leaves us free from any responsibility or effort to memorize. Students in my Hebrew classes who feel that they can depend upon the Holy Spirit to take the place of memorizing vocabulary soon discover the heretical nature of such a theory. Moreover, it does not mean that John's records of Jesus' teachings will be in the exact words that Jesus used. Six decades had perhaps taken away some of the words, but had added understanding and depth of meaning. "Memory, reflection, and the incubative work of the Spirit enabled the writer to penetrate to the heart of the Lord's person and mission and so elicit truth which he perceived only dimly, if at all, in his earlier days."[3]

Jesus had said also, "I will pray the Father, and he will give you another Counselor, to be with you for ever, even the Spirit of truth" (John 14:16,17). John had lived long enough to see the forces of falsehood begin to oppose the truth of the gospel. Men were denying that Jesus was the Christ, that He was possessed of the Father (I John 2:22,23); men were teaching that gratification of the fleshly appetites was not sin, that the fleshly nature of man was not real, that only the spiritual nature was real (I John 3:4-9); men were teaching that the Son of God could not therefore have taken a true human nature (I John 4:2,3). But the Holy Spirit, the Third Person of the Godhead who was sent to dwell in all who believe in Christ, is the Spirit of truth. He was the source of John's spiritual discernment of truth and error (I John 4:13; 5-7; cf. 2:26,27).

Some will say that this is not a very sure defense of truth; that it is too "subjective," and cannot be trusted. Two things need to be kept in mind: The Spirit who guides us in truth, who helps us discern between truth and error, is the same Spirit who inspired the Holy Scriptures; therefore truth will always be consonant with Scripture. In the second place, the guidance of the Spirit today extends to the entire Church, hence every individual is obligated to check his spiritual discernment with that of other Christians—including those of previous generations whose testimony is recorded in the great creeds and theological works of Christendom.

Jesus had further said concerning the Spirit, "And when he comes, he will convince the world of sin and of righteousness and of judgment" (John 16:8). He is the *Holy* Spirit, or the Spirit of holiness. John had had many years in which to learn the lessons of holiness. He knew that Jesus had once told Nicodemus, "Unless one is born of water and the Spirit, he cannot enter the kingdom of God" (John 3:5). He knew that access to the Kingdom under the symbol of the Holy City was denied to all evildoers (Revelation 21:8; 22:15). He knew that "any one born of God does not sin, but He who was born of God keeps him, and the evil one does not touch him" (I John 5:18). To John this was no mere academic discussion. He knew from experience that the One who was most completely possessed of the Holy Spirit could not be convicted of any sin. Jesus was holy as God was holy, and the Holy Spirit was the Spirit of Jesus.

Yet once more, Jesus had said, "When the Counselor comes, whom I shall send to you from the Father, even the Spirit of truth, who proceeds from the Father, he will bear witness to me" (John 15:26). The Spirit does not witness to Himself. For this reason Christians sometimes ask, "How do I know whether I have the Holy Spirit?" The Spirit witnesses to Jesus, just as the apostles witnessed to Jesus (cf. John 15:27).

The Holy Spirit is no mere doctrine: He is an experience. Every Christian in the Early Church knew that he possessed the Spirit of God, for he had an experience of the presence of the Spirit. That very same Spirit who dwelt in Jesus dwells in you and me, and we know it—or else He is not present (I John 3:24). He works through the Scriptures as we read or meditate upon them. He reminds us of God's will when we are tempted to wander away into sin. He tells us of Christ and His redeeming work. He warns us of error when we hear some false gospel. He helps us discern between error and truth. He does all these things—if we let Him. But we must learn to become sensitive to His leading. The apostle John had developed that sensitivity; that is why John was Christlike, for he had let the Spirit of Christ dwell in him. Did John speak in tongues? Did he have the gift of healing? Very little is said about these gifts in connection with John. But he did have the best gift of the Spirit, the gift of love. He learned that "if God so loved us, we also ought to love one another" (I John 4:11). In fact, "Love one another" could be described as John's life-text.

John and the Son of God. John was one of the first to heed the words of John the Baptist and follow Jesus (John 1:35-39). John was the last (and perhaps the only) disciple at the foot of the cross (John 19:26). Between those two events, John was with Jesus during most of His ministry. As one of the "inner circle" of the apostles (Peter, James, and John), he witnessed some of Jesus' works and experiences that the rest of the Twelve did not behold. Perhaps that is why he was the first to believe in the resurrection (John 20:8).

Son of God! John walked with Him, lived with Him, listened to Him. John heard Him make statements that sounded like the great "I Am": Jehovah Himself (cf. John 8:58). John saw Him perform miracles the like of which the world had never heard (cf. John 9:32). John heard Him pray in Gethsemane. John saw Him die on Calvary. John saw the gravecloths in the empty tomb. And John wrote, "The Word became flesh and dwelt among us, full of grace and truth; we have beheld his glory, glory as of the only Son from the Father" (John 1:14), and again, "That which was from the beginning, which we have heard, which we have seen with our eyes, which we have looked upon and touched with our hands . . . that which we have seen and heard we proclaim also to you, so that you may have fellowship with us; and our fellowship is with the Father and with his Son Jesus Christ"(I John 1:1,3).

To John the essence of antichrist was the denial of the Sonship of Jesus Christ: "Who is the liar but he who denies that Jesus is the Christ? This is the antichrist, he who denies the Father and the Son" (cf. I John 2:18-24). To John the great divide was the witness to the incarnation: "Every spirit which confesses that Jesus Christ has come in the flesh is of God, and every spirit which does not confess Jesus is not of God" (I John 4:2,3).

To John the way God made His love known to the world was the incarnation: "In this the love of God was made manifest among us, that God sent his only Son into the world, so that we might live through him" (I John 4:9). The propitiation for our sins, the satisfaction of divine justice necessary because of our guilt, the removal of divine wrath against all unrighteousness, was possible only by the act of God's love: "In this is love, not that we loved God but that he loved us and sent his Son to be the expiation [or better, propitiation][4] for our sins" (I John 4:10). "He appeared to take away sins, and in him there is no sin" (I John 3:5).

John wrote his Gospel to set forth his convictions: "these are written that you may believe that Jesus is the Christ, the Son of God, and that believing you may have life in his name" (John 20:31). Some would tell us that the Son of God of the Fourth Gospel is not the simple Carpenter of the Synoptics. But did John make Jesus, or did Jesus make John? Did the son of Zebedee turn the Carpenter of Nazareth into the Son of God, or did the One who came that we might have life turn the Galilean fisherman into the

157

holy theologian? For myself, I find it easier to believe the second alternative.

John and God the Father. In the symbolism of the Christian Church, John is often portrayed as an eagle, which is meant to imply that as the eagle is said to be the only bird able to look directly into the sun, so the apostle John is the only evangelist able to look directly upon God. I am not sure that either the symbolic identification or the explanation is true—but there is a great truth behind the symbolism. Philip spoke for all of us: "Lord, show us the Father, and we shall be satisfied." Jesus answered, "He who has seen me has seen the Father" (cf. John 14:8,9). John has attempted to portray Jesus in such a way that we shall see the Father. It can be summarized, I think, in one word: love.

"God so loved the world that he gave his only Son, that whoever believes in him should not perish but have eternal life. For God sent the Son into the world, not to condemn the world, but that the world might be saved through him" (John 3:16,17). Love is the only sufficient reason for the redemptive work of God in Christ. You and I have no claim on God. He owes us nothing. We are not by natural birth His children— that is a Stoic idea that has forced its way into Christian (or should we say sub-Christian?) thought. At this point the scientist is absolutely right when he ridicules the notion that man—a microscopically insignificant bit of the vast universe—should presume to identify himself with the Creator. But what the scientist has not been able to discover, God has revealed in Jesus Christ: God loves us. And by receiving this incarnation of God's love into our hearts and lives, we can become God's children (cf. John 1:12).

Only love is sufficient to explain the sacrifice of Jesus. Why did God let His Son die? What kind of divine justice is it that allowed wicked men to torture and kill One who went about doing only good? Or was God unable to stop it? Men struggle with the problem, seeking an answer; but the answer that God has given is sufficient: He loved us, even while we were sinners. "In this the love of God was made manifest among us, that God sent his only Son into the world, so that we might live through him" (I John 4:9). Jesus willingly went to the cross because He knew that only in this way would the Father be glorified. "Now is my soul troubled. And what shall I say, 'Father, save me from this hour'? No, for this purpose I have come to this hour. Father, glorify thy name" (John 12:27,28). After John had pondered the mystery of divine condescension for many years, he realized at last, "We have seen and testify that the Father has sent his Son as the Savior of the world. . . . So we know and believe the love God has for us" (I John 4:14,16).

Love is sufficient to express obedience to divine commandments. "This is my commandment, that you love one another as I have loved you. . . . This I command you, to love one another" (John 15:12, 17). Every law in the Decalogue can be obeyed by simply this: Love one another. The summary of the Law was expressed by Jesus in the two commandments: to love God, and to love your neighbor. John says, "Beloved, let us love one another; for love is of God, and he who loves is born of God and knows God. He who does not love does not know God; for God is love" (I John 4:7,8).

To John the example of divine love is sufficient to compel human love. "Beloved, if God so loved us, we also ought to love one another" (I John 4:11). To John the demonstration of love was a manifestation of God: "No man has ever seen God; if we love one another, God abides in us and his love is perfected in us" (I John 4:12). In fact, so essential is the demonstration of love on our part that John writes with great emphasis, "If any one says, 'I love God,' and hates his brother, he is a liar, for he who does not love his brother whom he has seen, cannot love God whom he has not seen. And this commandment we have from him, that he who loves God should love his brother also" (I John 4:20,21).

This is John the theologian. Many have summarized his theology in the key words: light, life, love. Life, I think, would characterize what he tells us about the Holy Spirit, for He is the source of life. We are born anew by the Spirit. We live by the Spirit. We have holiness of life by the Spirit. Light characterizes the Son, the true Light that came into the world. In His light we see light. God the Father is invisible, but the Son has manifested Him. Love characterizes the Father. God is love. We do not even know God if we do not know what love is, and to say that we love God without loving our brother human being is hollow mockery. Yet these three are one, and what is said of any one Person can be said of the others. We therefore say that these three are one God.

You thought theology was supposed to be dry and lifeless? Not so. Theology brings God into daily life.

It derives concrete realizations from the abstract. It gathers together diverse teachings into useful categories and applies them to life situations. At least that is what John the theologian did with theology.

Notes

1. There is a different viewpoint, according to which the theologian is a philosopher. The difference, in my estimation, arises from a man's methodology: if he works at the problem from deductive processes and speculation, he is more of the philosopher; if he works inductively from what God has revealed, he is more of the scientist.

2. This is not the place to enter into a discussion of the Johannine problems. I am personally convinced that the simplest and most satisfactory solution to the problem is to accept the traditional view that John the son of Zebedee, the "disciple whom Jesus loved," wrote the Gospel of John, the Epistles, and the Apocalypse. This chapter proceeds on that assumption. For a discussion of the problem see R. V. G. Tasker, *The Gospel According to St. John* (Grand Rapids, Mich.: Wm. B. Eerdmans Publishing Co., 1960), pp. 11-20, and William Temple, *Readings in St. John's Gospel* (London: Macmillan and Co., 1950), pp. ix-xxxiii.

3. Everett F. Harrison, "The Gospel and the Gospels," *Bibliotheca Sacra* 116 (April, 1959), p. 114.

4. For a study of this great theme, and in particular the words used to describe it, see Leon Morris, *The Apostolic Preaching of the Cross* (Grand Rapids, Mich.: Wm. B. Eerdmans Publishing Co., 1955), pp. 125–185, especially pp. 177–180.

FOR FURTHER READING:
Author's selected bibliography

(A number of titles in my *Men Who Knew God* are likewise pertinent to the New Testament, such as Bible Dictionaries, Atlases, etc. I have not repeated them here in the interest of space.)

Bible Dictionaries (articles on persons, places, terms, etc.)

A Dictionary of the Bible, edited by James Hastings. New York: Charles Scribner's Sons, 1898 ff. 4 vols. and extra volume. [In spite of need of revision in many places, plus presuppositions that are questionable, this work is still valuable for its many excellent articles on New Testament subjects.]

A Dictionary of Christ and the Gospels, edited by James Hastings. New York: Charles Scribner's Sons, 1924. 2 vols. [Not so well known as the previous work, but in many respects superior for work in the Gospels. Some of the articles are the finest treatments of their respective subjects that I have found.]

A Dictionary of the Apostolic Church, edited by James Hastings. New York: Charles Scribner's Sons, 1915. 2 vols. [Probably the least known of the three titles given here and of somewhat lower quality. Still, when I was teaching The Beginnings of Christianity, I combed it thoroughly and found it amply rewarding.]

J. D. Douglas (ed.), *The New Bible Dictionary*. Grand Rapids: Wm. B. Eerdmans Publishing Co., 1962. 1375 pages, 16 plates, 17 maps. [The best one-volume Bible dictionary in English, in my opinion. Every student of the Bible should have a good, up-to-date Bible dictionary and should use it constantly. This one is conservative in theology, excellent in scholarship, and well produced.]

Baker's Dictionary of Theology, edited by Everett F. Harrison, Geoffrey W. Bromiley, and Carl F. H. Henry. Grand Rapids: Baker Book House, 1960. 566 pp. [A very useful volume for ready reference on any subject included by the broad term *theology*. The viewpoint is conservative but the scholarship is fully aware of competing views.]

L. H. Grollenberg, *Atlas of the Bible*. Translated by Joyce M. H. Reid and H. H. Rowley. New York: Thomas Nelson and Sons, 1956. 165 pp., 35 maps, 408 photographs. [My first choice for a Bible atlas, with excellent text, fine maps, and a splendid collection of pictures.]

L. H. Grollenberg, *Shorter Atlas of the Bible*. Translated by Mary F. Hedlund. New York: Thomas Nelson & Sons, 1960. 195 pp. [This is a condensed version of the atlas which I have recommended most highly. Get the larger edition if you can afford it.]

The Macmillan Bible Atlas, ed. by Y. Aharoni and M. Avi-Yonah. New York: Macmillan, 1968. 184 pp. including 284 maps, tables, indexes. [A wonderful set of maps, with an individual map for almost every significant event in the Bible. Not much descriptive text, but occasional pictures of archeological discoveries or inscriptions that add background. You'll use it all the time!]

Paul Bruin and Philipp Giegel. *Jesus Lived Here*. Translated by William Neil. New York: William Morrow and Company, 1958. 239 pp. [A splendid collection of photographs to help you visualize the Holy Land.]

Charles F. Pfeiffer, *Baker's Bible Atlas*. Grand Rapids: Baker Book House, 1961. 333 pages, 26 maps in color, 18 maps in black and white, many photographs. [A very good atlas, for those who simply cannot afford Grollenberg's *Atlas of the Bible*.]

Art and Literature

George Ferguson, *Signs & Symbols in Christian Art*. 2d edition. New York: Oxford University Press, 1955. 346 pp., 96 plates, XV color plates. [The symbols are illustrated by line drawings alongside the text; arrangement is by subject; the plates provide a general introduction to the great religious art of the Renaissance.]

Cynthia Pearl Maus, *Christ and the Fine Arts*. 5th edition. New York: Harper & Brothers, 1938. 764 pp. [A storehouse of illustrative material in pictures, poetry, music, and stories.]

The Story of Jesus in the World's Literature, edited by Edward Wagenknecht, illustrations by Fritz Kredel. New York: Creative Age Press, Inc., 1946. 479 pp. [A fine selection, arranged by subjects.]

Daily Life in Ancient Times

Roland de Vaux, *Ancient Israel: Its Life and Institutions*. Translated by John McHugh. London: Darton, Longman & Todd, 1961. xxiii, 592 pages. [This is the work of a Roman Catholic scholar who has spent most of his life in Jerusalem. The contents include family institutions, civil institutions, military institutions, and religious institutions. In addition to Biblical material, the author includes quantities of other information, particularly from the daily life of the Arabs. It is a most thorough work, and its bibliography is almost exhaustive on every subject.]

William Sanford LaSor, *Daily Life in Bible Times*. Cincinnati: Standard Publishing Co., 1966. 128 pp.

Everyday Life in Bible Times. Washington, D.C.: National Geographic Society, 1967. 448 pp., 528 illustrations (412 in color), 13 maps. [An exquisite work.]

A Dictionary of Life in Bible Times, by W. Corswant, completed and illustrated by Edouard Urech, translated by Arthur Heathcote. New York: Oxford University Press, 1960. 309 pp. [An excellent work to help bring the Biblical characters to life.]

A. C. Bouquet, *Everyday Life in New Testament Times*. New York: Charles Scribner's Sons, 1954. xix, 236 pages, 102 illustrations. [Somewhat different in arrangement from the present work. The emphasis is more on the life of the Greco-Roman world. The illustrations are helpful.]

Archeology

Jack Finegan, *Light from the Ancient Past; the Archeological Background of Judaism and Christianity*. 2d ed., Princeton: Princeton University Press, 1959. xxxvii, 638 pages, 204 illustrations, 6 maps, 4 plans. [A most valuable work, containing all of the significant historical data of the ancient Middle East, with an incredible amount of reference material in the footnotes.]

G. Ernest Wright, *Biblical Archaeology*. Abridged edition. Philadelphia: Westminster Press, 1960. 198 pp. [A condensation, in an inexpensive edition, of the larger work by the same title.]

John A Thompson, *Archaeology and the New Testament*. Grand Rapids: Wm. B. Eerdmans Publishing Co., 1960. 151 pp. [This and the preceding title are brief but reliable works.]

William M. Ramsay, *The Bearing of Recent Discovery on the Trustworthiness of the New Testament*. 2d edition. London: Hodder and Stoughton, 1915; reprinted 1953 by Baker Book House, Grand Rapids. [Sir William Ramsay wrote many books and articles and I cannot begin to list the important ones here. I have selected this title because it gives the author's summary of the results of his life's work. Unfortunately, Ramsay's works lack splendid organization, and the scholar has to roam through many of Ramsay's works to find material on any desired subject. We are indebted to Baker Book House for reprinting several of the more important titles.]

The Background of Judaism

George Foot Moore, *Judaism*. Cambridge, Mass.: Harvard University Press, 1927. 2 vols. [The classic on the subject of Judaism in the first centuries of the Christian era.]

Josephus. Complete Works, translated by William Whiston. Grand Rapids: Kregel Publications, 1960 (reprint). [The serious New Testament student should often look into Josephus for insights and sidelights. A bit of a critical approach to Josephus is, of course, necessary.]

Robert H. Pfeiffer, *History of New Testament Times*. New York: Harper & Brothers, 1949. 561 pp. [Valuable for a study of the intertestamental period and its literature; the work contains a magnificent bibliography.]

Floyd V. Filson, *The New Testament against Its Environment*. (Studies in Biblical Theology, No. 3.) London: S C M Press Ltd., 1950. 103 pp. [An excellent summary of the background of the New Testament, with footnote references to the significant publications.]

Life of Christ

A Harmony of the Gospels, edited by William Arnold Stevens and Ernest de Witt Burton. Boston: Silver, Burdett & Company, 1897. 237 pp. [I fail to understand how anyone can study the life of Christ without a harmony of the Gospels. This one uses the text of 1881 (English Revised Version), but in my opinion its arrangement of the events in the four Gospels is superior.]

Ralph D. Heim, *A Harmony of the Gospels for Students*. Philadelphia: Muhlenberg Press, 1947. 209 pp. [Uses the *RSV* text.]

Alfred Edersheim, *The Life and Times of Jesus the Messiah*. Eleventh impression. London: Longmans, Green and Co., 1901. 2 vols. [In many ways, still the best life of Christ. There seems to be no inclination in modern scholarship to attempt a synthesis of the subject as Edersheim has done; yet much in Edersheim needs to be revised or rejected.]

William Manson, *Jesus the Messiah*. (The Synoptic Tradition of the Revelation of God in Christ, with Special Reference to Form Criticism.) Philadelphia: Westminster Press, 1946. 267 pp. [Useful for an understanding of how the Gospel record is handled by modern form critics; Manson is quite a conservative representative of modern scholarship.]

J. Gresham Machen, *The Virgin Birth of Christ*. New York: Harper

& Brothers, 1930. 415 pp. [A classic. The scholar who ignores this work lays himself open to the charge either of ignorance or of unwillingness to face the facts as presented by the best of conservative scholarship.]

G. Campbell Morgan, *The Crises of the Christ*. New York: Fleming H. Revell Co., 1903. 477 pp. [One of the finest works by one of the greatest of recent Bible expositors. Everyone who teaches or seriously studies the life of Christ should read this work not once but often.]

G. Campbell Morgan, *The Teaching of Christ*. New York: Fleming H. Revell Co., 1913. 333 pp. [An excellent study; there are, however, areas of Christ's teachings that are not covered.]

Everett F. Harrison, *A Short Life of Christ*. Grand Rapids: Wm. B. Eerdmans Publishing Co., 1968. 287 pp. [A beautiful and reverent life of Christ, undergirded by deep scholarship, but written for the layman.]

A. B. Bruce, *The Training of the Twelve*. 3d edition. New York: Richard R. Smith, Inc., 1930. 552 pp. [A well-known and highly praised work that is rich in its insights.]

Richard Chenevix Trench, *Notes on the Parables of Our Lord*. 8th edition. New York: D. Appleton & Company, 1856. 425 pp. [A classic, but why has no one given us an up-to-date study of the same proportions?]

Richard Chenevix Trench, *Notes on the Miracles of Our Lord*. Eleventh edition. London: Macmillan and Co., 1878. 515 pp. [Again, a classic, and very rich, but in need of revision.]

A. G. Hebert, *The Throne of David*. London: Faber and Faber, 1941. 277 pp. [A modern effort to deal with Christ in the typology of the Old Testament.]

H. V. Morton, *In the Steps of the Master*. 23d edition. London: Methuen & Co., 1953. 388 pp. [This is a beautiful combination of geography, travelogue, religious devotion, and interesting anecdotes. I have carried it with me in the steps of the Master, and the opinion I had previously formed about the work was not diminished.]

The Beginnings of Christianity

F. J. Foakes Jackson and Kirsopp Lake, editors, *The Beginnings of Christianity*. London: Macmillan and Co., 1922. 5 vols. [A masterful work, at some places based on presuppositions which I not only cannot accept but which I feel are unwarranted. Nevertheless, it must be studied—particularly the first volume—by anyone working in Acts.]

F. F. Bruce, *A Commentary on the Book of Acts.* (The New International Commentary on the New Testament.) Grand Rapids: Wm. B. Eerdmans Publishing Co., 1956. 555 pp. [Of all the commentaries on Acts I have used, this is in many ways the most satisfactory. The scholarship is massive; the viewpoint is conservative; the application is devotional and helpful.]

J. Gresham Machen, *The Origin of Paul's Religion.* London: Hodder and Stoughton, 1921. 329 pp. [A thorough work on a subject that perhaps does not claim the attention today that it did formerly. Nevertheless, many of the points in this book are still valid and need to be repeated for the problems of Pauline study that are raised today.]

Bernard Ramm, *The Witness of the Spirit.* Grand Rapids: Wm. B. Eerdmans Publishing Co., 1960. 140 pp. [A fine study of the Holy Spirit and His place in the believer's life.]

F. F. Bruce, *The New Testament Documents: Are They Reliable?* 5th revised edition. Grand Rapids: Wm. B. Eerdmans Publishing Co., 1960. 120 pp. [A useful handbook on the basic problems of New Testament introduction, from a conservative and scholarly viewpoint.]

H. V. Morton, *In the Steps of St. Paul.* New York: Dodd, Mead & Company, 1955. 499 pp. [Originally published in 1936, this work, like Morton's companion volume on the Master, is charming. It contains quantities of background material, unfortunately without documentation— which annoys the scholar who wants to know where he got some of his material.]

Word Studies

Leon Morris, *The Apostolic Preaching of the Cross.* Grand Rapids: Wm. B. Eerdmans Publishing Co., 1955. 296 pp. [A splendid work, combining thoroughly scholarly word studies, well-founded theology, and deep devotion. Highly recommended!]

J. J. von Allmen, *Vocabulary of the Bible.* English translation by a group of scholars, edited by Hilda A. Wilson. London: Lutterworth Press, 1958. 479 pp. [Contains a breadth of scholarship. When studying words we need to be reminded that the context governs the meaning of words at least as much as the reverse. Always study words in context!]